GOH KENG SWEE
on CHINA
Selected Essays

GOH KENG SWEE
on CHINA
Selected Essays

Edited by

Zheng Yongnian
John Wong

East Asian Institute, National University of Singapore, Singapore

 **World Scientific**

NEW JERSEY · LONDON · SINGAPORE · BEIJING · SHANGHAI · HONG KONG · TAIPEI · CHENNAI

Published by

World Scientific Publishing Co. Pte. Ltd.
5 Toh Tuck Link, Singapore 596224
USA office: 27 Warren Street, Suite 401-402, Hackensack, NJ 07601
UK office: 57 Shelton Street, Covent Garden, London WC2H 9HE

Library of Congress Cataloging-in-Publication Data
Goh, Keng Swee, 1918–2010.
    Goh Keng Swee on China : selected essays / edited by Zheng Yongnian, John Wong.
    p. cm.
    Includes index.
    ISBN 978-9814407236
    1. China--Economic conditions--1976–2000. 2. China--Economic policy--1976–2000.
I. Zheng, Yongnian. II. Wong, John, 1939–   III. Title.
    HC427.92.G632 2013
    330.951'059--dc23

                                                                2012035457

British Library Cataloguing-in-Publication Data
A catalogue record for this book is available from the British Library.

Copyright © 2013 by World Scientific Publishing Co. Pte. Ltd.

All rights reserved. This book, or parts thereof, may not be reproduced in any form or by any means, electronic or mechanical, including photocopying, recording or any information storage and retrieval system now known or to be invented, without written permission from the Publisher.

For photocopying of material in this volume, please pay a copying fee through the Copyright Clearance Center, Inc., 222 Rosewood Drive, Danvers, MA 01923, USA. In this case permission to photocopy is not required from the publisher.

In-house Editor: DONG Lixi

Typeset by Stallion Press
Email: enquiries@stallionpress.com

Printed in Singapore.

About the Editors

ZHENG Yongnian is Professor and Director of the East Asian Institute (EAI) at the National University of Singapore. He received his BA and MA degrees from Beijing University, and his PhD from Princeton University. He was a recipient of Social Science Research Council-MacArthur Foundation Fellowship (1995–1997) and John D and Catherine T MacArthur Foundation Fellowship (2003–2004). He was Professor and founding Research Director of the China Policy Institute, the University of Nottingham, United Kingdom. Professor Zheng is the editor of Series on Contemporary China (World Scientific Publishing), China Policy Series (Routledge), *China: An International Journal* and *East Asian Policy*. His papers have appeared in journals such as *Comparative Political Studies, Political Science Quarterly* and *China Quarterly*. He is also the author and editor of numerous books. Besides his research work, Professor Zheng has also been an academic activist. He served as a consultant to United Nation Development Programme on China's rural development and democracy.

John WONG is currently Professorial Fellow and Academic Advisor at the EAI, National University of Singapore. He was formerly Research Director of EAI and Director of the Institute of East Asian Political Economy. He taught Economics at the University of Hong Kong from 1966 to 1970 and at the National University of Singapore from 1970 to 1990. He has held short-term visiting positions at Harvard, Yale, Oxford and Toronto. He obtained his PhD from the University of London in 1966. He has written/edited 33 books, and published over 400 articles and chapters on China and other East Asian economies, including ASEAN. In addition, he has written over 80 policy-related reports on China's development for the Singapore government.

Contents

Introduction

Most of the papers in this collection were written by Goh Keng Swee around the early 1990s, with the exception of the first chapter, "China's Economic Policies in a Historical Perspective", which was his speech delivered at a conference for foreign investors in 1987. By that time, Goh was already an economic adviser to China's State Council on the opening up of China's coastal cities and on tourism development. As an economic adviser to China's top leadership (1985–1990), he was able to have access to important information on China's development as well as observe changes on the ground at a close range. Consequently, he had developed not just a good grasp of the structure and operation of the Chinese economy, but also a strong interest in modern Chinese studies.

After his return to Singapore from China in 1990, Goh continued to be fascinated by China's latest developments, particularly the challenges faced by China in its transition from a socialist economy to a market system. He therefore took immediate steps to reorganise the Institute of East Asian Philosophies (IEAP), which he founded in 1983 to promote Confucian ethics for his Moral Education programme, and changed its research direction from Confucian and religious studies to research on the political, economic and social development of contemporary China, or "China watching" in short. For this mission, he appointed John Wong as director of IEAP in 1990, which was renamed the Institute of East Asian Political Economy (IEAPE) in 1992.

Goh remained the chairman of IEAPE, which was to operate as a "think tank" on China for the Singapore government. Thus, IEAPE's major research focus was on China's economic reform and its political and social changes, with most of its research activities primarily policy-oriented. Zheng Yongnian joined IEAPE as a research fellow in 1996.

1

He was IEAPE's first trained political scientist with a PhD from an American Ivy-League university. Up till then, IEAPE's political analysts were formerly officials or cadres of the Chinese government, none with a PhD. In 1997, IEAPE was again reconstituted to become East Asian Institute (EAI) and function as a full-time autonomous research organisation within the National University of Singapore. In a way, both Wong and Zheng are familiar with the background of Goh's writings as put together here, particularly for Wong, who had worked closely with Goh during that period.

It should be noted that the early 1990s was a time of great political and economic uncertainty in China since Deng Xiaoping introduced economic reform and the open-door policy in 1979. Politically, both the Chinese government and the people were still recovering from the shock of the Tiananmen crackdown in June 1989. Economically, the market reform was at a crossroads. China started the reform process with a successful breakthrough in rural and agricultural reform in the first part of the 1980s before moving into industrial reform in the urban areas after the mid-1980s, which had proved to be exceedingly difficult. The resulting dual-tracked price system had become very hard to administer, giving rise to high inflation and widespread *guan-dao* (rent-seeking) activities. And this led to the outbreak of the Tiananmen protest.

By the early 1990s, China landed with a messy, half-reformed economy, with all its well-known problems, ranging from market distortions caused by price controls to the economic inefficiency of its SOEs (state-owned enterprises), and from the need for the reform of the tax system to the need for setting a more clear-cut relationship between central and local governments. All these became a familiar refrain in Goh's writings. He was particularly concerned about the unfinished business of economic reform in China. He pointed out, quite rightly, that the most crucial area of reform for China in the next phase would be the SOE reform and banking reform, with the two being closely interrelated.

Looking back, Deng Xiaoping's *Nanxun* (tour of South China) in February 1992 was the real turning point in China's reform when Deng openly called for a bold approach to reform in order to realise the "socialist market economy", and to further open up China to foreign trade and foreign investment. This had eventually given rise to two decades of double-digit rates of growth for the Chinese economy. Goh's papers were written around this time, either just shortly before or shortly after Deng's *Nanxun*. In all fairness, the long-term results of Deng's *Nanxun* were not immediately apparent to people at that time. In this sense, Goh did not have the benefit of the hindsight of this event.

Not surprisingly, Goh appeared quite pessimistic, as reflected in his writings, over the future course of China's reform. As a seasoned politician and a practical economist, he just could not see how China could possibly achieve a smooth and rapid breakthrough in reform in the short run, given the fact that the post-Tiananmen top leadership was basically dominated by ideologues and conservatives as typified in the person of Premier Li Peng. In fact, most China experts at that time, including many eminent American China-scholars, were basically thinking like Goh.

Western China-scholars were confronted by some of the fundamental "contradictions" underpinning China's reform. How would it be possible to reconcile the inherent conflict between the Marxist-Leninist political structure and the free market system? Thus, most Western China-scholars advocated democracy, or having a political reform to precede economic reform. But Goh was much more sanguine. He was more pragmatic. He tended to agree with Deng Xiaoping's doctrine of having economic reform first and political reform later. To Goh, it was much like having economic development first and democratisation later, as clearly exemplified by the successful East Asian development experience. He saw how the Russian reformers, in putting political *glasnost* before economic *perestroika*, had brought about the collapse of the Soviet Union.

As a practical economist himself, Goh naturally understood that democracy could very well complicate the reform process as too much politics would actually hamper the reform progress. What he wanted to see in China at that time was for the post-Tiananmen leadership to be more flexible and less rigid towards the operation of the market. He also wanted China to give higher priority to legal reform. To him, a more effective legal system and better governance would by far be more conducive to economic reform and development than any drastic political change.

With no hindsight, neither Goh nor many China scholars at that time could have foreseen how Deng Xiaoping had managed to make the Chinese Communist Party (CCP) so ideologically malleable as to readily embrace the market economy without much of a fuss. Deng in his *Nanxun* speech in Shenzhen (which was later issued by the CCP as the Central Document No. 2 for 1992) said: "If the Capitalist economies have a stock market, why can't a socialist system also have one? China should try it out...."). With such ideological flexibility, the CCP had no problem with a deeper and broader market reform. After the *Nanxun*, such a scenario of a Marxist-Leninist party constraining market reform had actually not happened in China. Nobody then would have ever foreseen that in 1997 President Jiang Zemin would take steps to amend the Party constitution in order to admit capitalists into the CCP!

As an economist, Goh was particularly bothered by the existence of too many inefficient SOEs in China. He kept harping on the SOE problems in his writings, partly also because he was very at home with this subject. He had personally been involved in the development and management of Singapore's equivalent (government-linked companies or GLCs) to China's SOEs.

China's SOEs operated much like a mini-welfare state, taking over the social welfare functions of the local community while providing each worker with an "iron rice bowl" (permanent employment). Reforming a big SOE would mean subjecting it to hard budget constraints (or profit maximisation), and this would inevitably involve the restructuring of its management and retrenchment of its workers. Goh once said: How could they sack the management staff who were their own Party cadres? How could they lay off workers without having first established the required social safety net? The CCP was supposed to be made up of the proletariat, who were supposed to be masters of society. Thus, he could well understand Li Peng's predicament in this, and he also knew that Li possessed no political will to tackle the fundamental problems of the

SOEs. Goh was actually right in his analysis, and many China experts at that time held similar views.

Looking back, not just Goh but all of us had underestimated China's ability and its ingenuity in tackling its own problems. After Li Peng, Zhu Rongji took over the job of reforming the SOEs. Zhu had the political will to do so, and he also had the imagination and patience for this task. Zhu's ways of reforming the SOEs included his strategy of *zhua-da fang-xiao* (concentrating on the strategically big SOEs and disposing of the many small ones) and his innovative *xia-gang* (off-post) tactics in dealing with redundant workers. This Chinese way of reforming SOEs was much more effective than the Big Bang approach adopted by Russia. History has proved this. But it was not obvious to Goh at that time.

Nor would Goh ever imagine that in 2012 the Industrial and Commercial Bank of China (ICBC) would become the world's largest bank by market capitalisation! Furthermore, the Chinese *reminbi* is on the way to become one of the world's leading international currencies.

In the early 1990s, the People's Bank of China (the central bank) basically operated much like a cashier to the central government, without having to carry out such essential duties as managing the country's monetary policy. All the other state banks did not function like commercial banks. Goh could see banking reform was as much a great challenge to China as its SOE reform. He did not expect Zhu to find a way to restructure and reform China's banking system — basically step by step — after China's accession to the WTO in 2001.

A question may then be posed: Was Goh a good "China scholar"? He could certainly be considered a great scholar in terms of what he had written. But he himself had never claimed to be a true China scholar in any strict academic sense.

We know that Goh was a first-rate economist in his own right. His tenure as an economic adviser to the Chinese government had given him access to a lot of background information and practical experience about the Chinese economy. His subsequent follow-up research on China had further increased his understanding of China. He had indeed gained good insights into how the Chinese economy at that time functioned. Modern scholarship tends to be highly specialised and technical. As economic adviser to the Chinese government, Goh had written a number of good reports on banking reform and price reform and so on, and these reports could have easily been converted into good books. By all these, one can justifiably describe him as a first-class "China expert".

China today is the world's second largest economy, and it is poised to overtake the United States as the world's largest economic entity within 10 years. China is holding the world's largest foreign reserves. In recent years, China sells more cars (18 million units) than the United States. Goh had long predicted the eventual rise of China. His logic was quite simple. If the Japanese had made it, and then the Koreans and the Taiwanese, why not the Chinese? But he had certainly not foreseen the rise of China in such a short span of time. No China expert at that time had ever imagined that the automobile age could have arrived in China so soon.

From the outset, Goh was acutely aware of the enormous challenges faced by foreign China experts. He would certainly be the first to admit that no outside China expert had ever correctly predicted China's future development. He had often cautioned scholars at the IEAPE with this advice: "Nobody knows what is going on inside *Zhongnanhai* (China's "White House", i.e. the compound in Beijing where top Chinese leaders live and work)". Such is the peril of "China watching" then and still now!

We must make haste to add that the failure of China experts in correctly predicting China's future outcome should in no way diminish the value of Goh's collected writings on China almost two decades on. To Singaporeans, this volume will add to what Goh, as one of Singapore's founding fathers, had achieved beyond his political career, apart from capturing the historical significance of his contributions to modern Chinese studies in Singapore. More importantly, Goh's analytical discussion of a wide range of problems and issues that were plaguing China's half-reformed economy at that time, together with his insights into possible remedies and policy options, would certainly be of great interest and usefulness to students researching on the transitional economy elsewhere. Here lies the book's intrinsic academic merit.

To facilitate the readers' better understanding of what Goh had written, we have added a short introduction to each chapter.

John Wong and Zheng Yongnian

I

China's Economic Policies in a Historical Perspective*

Editors' Note

Goh Keng Swee was addressing foreign investors in 1987 who were unfamiliar with the business environment in China and also unsure of China's reform policies — Would they stay? For a quick understanding of China's open-door policy historically, Goh said one need not go beyond 1793, a fateful year, when Emperor Qianlong summarily dismissed the British request (through Lord Macartney) to open up China for foreign trade. But, eventually China was forced by the Opium War to open its door, and that was accompanied by a century of foreign oppression and humiliation. This in turn led to the rise of the Communists to power in 1949, which closed China's door again until 1978.

Goh also cautioned foreign investors about the unfamiliar institutional structure in China's newly reformed economy, which gave rise to the dual-price system and many SOEs with non-market behaviour. Taking a more optimistic long-term view, Goh observed that China was in the final phase of its historical transformation from an ancient civilisation into a modern industrial state. This has come true today!

---

*Speech delivered on 22 October 1987 at the opening of the International Conference on "China's Foreign Trade and Investment Policies: Expectations and Opportunities".

The foreign businessman when contemplating business prospects in China experiences mixed feelings. First, he is dazzled at the prospect of the huge domestic market: one billion consumers. On getting down to the nitty gritty, he soon finds that things are not what they seem to be and he must rid himself of all kinds of preconceptions. The Chinese have their own methods of doing business and he must understand the system if he is going to get anywhere. So one way or another, he acquires the minimum knowledge. If he makes the right contact or has the right product, negotiations are successfully concluded. Then the real work begins. The operating environment is different from the one he is accustomed to. So a major adjustment has to be made in expectations, modes of assessment, methods of planning and in general psychological attitudes.

Throughout this period of adjustment, he is assailed by doubt, not only over small matters of detail but over the large issues. Is China serious about the policy of opening to the outside world? How can one be sure that the policies initiated by Deng Xiaoping will last beyond his departure from the political scene? How reliable are the accounts of the conflict between conservatives and reformers? What happens if the reformers lose? If the reformers win, is China introducing a form of capitalism?

Chinese leaders have gone to great lengths to give assurances that the reforms are here to stay and China will retain its socialist system. The frequency with which such assurances have been given suggests that a communication gap of some kind exists. One reason why the gap exists relates to differences in culture, and this leads to a state of mutual lack of comprehension. It is a human failing to believe that other people think, act and feel just as we do and we get puzzled when they give evidence to the contrary. I think this business of cultural difference can be overdone at the relatively high level of contact which business executives make. Business discussions center around prices, costs, profits, production and supply matters, and reason, rather than sentiment, determines the outcome.

In my view, the main reason for the communication gap is historical. It is trite but nevertheless true that the history of China proceeded differently in the last two or three thousand years from that of Europe or America. And, except for specialists, each side is more or less totally ignorant of the history of the other. To understand China, some understanding of recent, if not ancient history, is a must. This is because the Chinese people have a keener sense of their own history than can be said of most contemporary societies.

Recorded Chinese history extends for more than three thousand years. For most of the period it is a story of a self-contained civilization developing a unique culture and political system. For the purpose of understanding China's policy of opening to the outside world, however, we need not go beyond the year 1793. That was the fateful year in which Lord Macartney called upon the Chinese Emperor Qianlong with the request from his monarch, King George III, that the celestial kingdom open its doors to trade with the outside world.

The British envoy was received by the Qing emperor Qianlong in his summer residence. But his request for the opening of regular trade and the stationing of a mission in the capital was rejected. Qianlong was a strong emperor and the Qing dynasty had reached its peak under him. In refusing Lord Macartney's proposal on trade ties, Qianlong was reaffirming the traditional Chinese view that the empire was self-sufficient in all the requirements of the people and had no need of the manufactures of the West. Thus the doors to trade with the outside world were closed. It took five more decades before the doors were forcibly opened.

It may be interesting to compare China's early contact with the West with Japan's experience. Japan's first brush with the West came in a less pleasant form than a visiting aristocrat. In 1853, the United States dispatched Commodore Perry's warships to Tokyo with the demand that the country be opened to trade. Unlike China of 1793, Japan's government, that of the Tokugawa shogunate, was tottering on its last legs. In 1858, it signed a treaty for setting up ports through which the Japanese would trade with the outside world. There is a widespread belief that unlike the Chinese, the Japanese willingly acquiesced to Western demands. This is untrue. The signing of the Treaty outraged public opinion, and the Minister who signed it was assassinated and the foreigners were frequently attacked. However, after two naval bombardments in 1863 and 1864, the Japanese bowed to the inevitable.

Japan was fortunate in having a small group of young samurai of remarkable ability, vision and daring. The oldest was Tomomi Iwakura, 43 years old, and the youngest, Hirobumi Ito, 27 years old. This group laid the foundation of modern Japan. Having disposed of the last Shogun and restored the Meiji emperor, 55 of them set out on an extraordinary voyage of discovery of Western countries. In all, they spent two years abroad, studying all important aspects of Western societies — their constitutions, their legal systems, their schools and universities, their industries and their armies and navies. Thus, over the next 30 or 40 years, the core of Japan's political leadership was equipped with an accurate understanding of Western government and economic systems. This knowledge enabled them to correctly assess the policy recommendations of their experts on how to restructure their country in gradual stages, and eventually to join the ranks of modern industrial states. Japan's historic experience has taught her people the necessity of acquiring comprehensive and accurate knowledge as the basis of decisions on policy and action. Western scholars studying Japan's recent spectacular economic successes have linked these to her unrivalled skills in collecting, analysing and disseminating information. The Japanese thus successfully applied the counsel of China's ancient strategist Sun-zi. He said, "Know yourself, know the other side and you can fight a hundred battles without danger." By contrast, the Qing government leaders had little understanding of the Western world and blundered from one disaster to another to its final collapse in 1911.

The forcible opening of doors to foreign trade in China took place as a consequence of two wars waged by foreign powers. These were the First Opium War, 1839–42, and the Second Opium War, 1856–60. These events ushered in a long era of great misfortune and calamity for the Chinese people. The disasters that befell the country were less the immediate consequences of the wars than the result of the decline of the central authority leading to disorder. Nor did the opening of China's market to foreign trade bring lasting economic benefits to foreign countries. For trade to prosper and bring mutual benefit to trading partners, a key requirement is economic progress under a stable and orderly government. That did not occur in China.

When the dynasty collapsed in 1911, events in China took their accustomed historical course. Warring factions battled for supremacy. But history introduced a new element in the struggle — the invasion of foreign powers. All these increased the misfortunes and suffering of the Chinese people. After 38 years of strife, China was once again reunited under the victorious Communist Party in 1949. The period of disorder was not exceptionally long by Chinese historical standards but the scale of conflict reached unprecedented heights. The two groups contending for mastery over China — the Communists and the Kuomintang — between them commanded more than eight million regular forces in the final battles. In Japan, by contrast, the Tokugawa shogunate was overthrown by 6,000 rebel soldiers and the issue was decided in a battle which lasted one afternoon. I make this comparison to emphasise the point that China is a large country with a complex social and political structure. What is accomplished in an afternoon in one country may take a longer time in China.

When the Communist Party leaders addressed their minds to the tasks facing them in 1949, the challenges appeared formidable. The devastation caused by decades of war had to be repaired. The country was short of infrastructure of every description — roads, railways, ports, telecommunication facilities and power — and lacked a modern industrial base. Even more important than inadequate physical structures was the neglected state of the schools, technical colleges and universities. Because of the international situation, the only source of technical and financial assistance was the Soviet Union. In the 1950s, China began a massive construction effort and adopted the Russian system of planning and controls.

The restoration of peace, unity and order provided a favourable setting for very rapid economic progress in the first decade. Despite the ultra-leftist errors committed in subsequent years, economic growth and, in particular, industrial expansion continued at a robust pace. But eventually, both the political leaders and the economic experts detected certain weaknesses and flaws in the system. By 1978, a consensus was reached within the Central Committee of the Communist Party that a thorough reform of economic policies must be undertaken. Confining my observations to the shortcomings as perceived by China's leaders, I shall describe some of the policies adopted to overcome these shortcomings and discuss some of their implications for foreign investment.

As China is a socialist country, all the major enterprises are state-owned. In practice, ownership and control may be vested in a variety of government agencies. The most common are the production ministries such as Ministry of Textile Industry, Ministry of Electronics Industry, Ministry of Light Industry, Ministry of Chemical Industry and Ministry of Metallurgical Industry. These may be central ministries of the central government or they may be their equivalents in provincial governments or even municipal government. Sometimes, enterprises owned by a central ministry may be transferred to a provincial or even city authority for better supervision and control. Sometimes, an enterprise may be owned by one of the large national trading companies or their provincial or even city equivalents.

Whatever the ownership arrangements, before the recent reforms got underway, all large enterprises had to arrange their production activities according to a plan determined by the State Planning Commission. The plan set physical targets for the output mix, specified quality standards, regulated the prices and provided for the necessary inputs in respect of quantity, quality and prices. The task of the enterprises was to make the best use of materials, labour, energy and other planned inputs to meet the production targets. The system had both advantages and disadvantages.

In the early years of reconstruction, the advantages were evident. It was an effective method of mobilising production skills in the form of engineering and scientific staffs to concentrate on what the Planning Commission rated as national priorities, such as building railways, exploiting mineral resources and manufacturing machinery. Despite the extensive criticism the system was subject to in recent years, it produced an extensive network of industries. There was hardly any product which China used that was not manufactured in China: intercontinental ballistic missiles (ICBMs), trucks, locomotives, machine tools, textiles, consumer electronics and other consumer goods. But the products generally suffered from inadequacies of two kinds. First, the quantity produced was insufficient and second, the design of these products was often outdated.

Insufficient output may be ascribed to China's large population and the chaos prevailing for a hundred years prior to 1949. Given time and the accumulation of physical capital, shortages could eventually be overcome by expanding production facilities. But out-of-date design, especially in the production of machinery and transport equipment, was a more serious matter. The reason was that the system of production, according to state plans, laid more stress on physical output than quality and up-to-date design. Enterprises had no incentive to introduce better design unless instructed to do so. Once a model of a commodity had been sanctioned for production, neither the enterprise nor the production ministry in charge felt any compelling motivation to improve on the design. Such innovations might require a new set of tools that might slow down current production. Or new components might be needed which were difficult to acquire, such as micro-electronic devices.

Since whatever was produced by the enterprise was taken away by a state agency, it could be irrational business practice to introduce improved products especially if this raised problems of sourcing of components and difficult negotiations with the Price Bureau for higher prices. Troubles of this kind are not peculiar to China; they affect the economies of Eastern Europe. So far as the production of consumer goods is concerned, weakness of this kind seems inherent in centrally planned economies.

China's leaders and economic experts recognized the limitations of central planning when applied in a rigid manner. They correctly identified the root weakness of the system, which comprised the important links between prominent components of the economy being either missing or existing in an inadequate form. In particular, they noted that production was not properly related to consumer demand, prices to costs, wages and salaries to performance and profits to enterprise efficiency. Thus they traced the waste and inefficiency of the system to one or more of these deficiencies.

The analysis and diagnosis were clearly correct, but it represented a courageous departure from the conventional wisdom of that time. This breakthrough was made possible as a result of both the pragmatic nature of the Chinese culture as well as Deng Xiaoping's constant reminder "to learn truth from facts". The media in China, both popular and academic, published frank accounts of faults in economic management. Hence, the feeling was widespread that something needed to be done. The remedies proposed had to consider economic logic on the one hand and, on the other, the institutional arrangements pertaining to production. Let us first consider logic. If the faults arose from improper links cited — between production and consumer demand, prices and costs, etc. — logic requires that market conditions should be given prominence in economic decisions. It is a simple matter to prescribe abstract principles about how to allow markets to determine outputs, prices, costs, wages and salaries, profits, etc. However, when it comes to determining policies applicable to the real situation in China, we must take into account the institutional arrangements concerning production. This means going back to the ownership and control of enterprises. These are organised along different lines from those in free enterprises. The large enterprises are more than production units. In the course of their evolution, they have come to provide for the employees not only permanent employment but an extensive range of welfare benefits — such as health and hospital services, subsidized housing (virtually free), pensions, schools and even universities for children of employees. Under the old system, the entire profits of the enterprise went to the owners, that is, the state; likewise when losses were made, because the enterprise produced goods whose prices had to be kept low, they were made good out of the state budget. The enterprise thus functioned like a government department, producing whatever it was ordered to produce with the materials supplied by the state.

Institutional arrangements of this kind place a constraint on the pace at which market forces can be allowed to determine economic decisions. For instance, it is not feasible to charge economic rents for accommodation provided at low rents to employees unless the employees are given corresponding pay increases. Nor is it possible to withdraw the status of permanent employment from those granted such status.

Another marked difference between Chinese enterprises and ours relates to the sharing of authority within the enterprise. Again for historical reasons, professional managers have to share authority with the Party apparatus and the trade union representatives. This arrangement goes back to the revolutionary years when the Party administered large areas of China while fighting the Kuomintang and/or Japanese armies. In the sometimes fluid battle situation, enterprise managers needed a stiffening of resolve. This was what the Party and trade union leaders provided. Once their participation in enterprise management has been institutionalized, it is not feasible to dismantle the system completely. Under a political system in which the supremacy of the Party is elevated to a cardinal principle, the disengagement of the Party from enterprise affairs will not be an easy matter to bring about.

Clearly, these complicated institutional issues affect the rate of reforms. There are also major economic policy constraints, the foremost of which concerns the impact of economic liberalisation on prices. One of the outcomes of centrally planned and directed system of production of previous years was price stability. As a result of prolonged control over prices and wages, these remained virtually unchanged for 30 years after the war. It is true that price controls were accompanied by extensive rationing of basic necessities, foodstuffs, clothing, etc. But prices were very low by world standards. The same applied to a wide range of raw materials and semi-finished goods, many of which were sold at a fraction of world prices.

Allowing market forces to determine prices runs the risk of an unacceptable rate of inflation if liberalisation proceeds at too fast a pace. A population accustomed to 30 years of price stability would take poorly to widespread price increases. But not to move fast enough would limit the benefits of reform in several ways. Incomplete reform of prices means that a part of the output of a product is sold through planned distribution channels at planned prices. Another part of the output may be sold by the producer to authorized buyers at negotiated prices. The balance of the output may be sold freely at whatever the market can bear. This leads to a multitiered price system. One undesirable effect of this on enterprise efficiency is that the profits of the enterprise may depend more critically on access to controlled supplies than on superior management. Enterprises with substantial access to planned supplies may be tempted to use excessive amounts of raw materials per unit of output. Multiple pricing has other bad effects. Management resources will be lavished on cultivating right connections, on preparing favourable negotiating positions to the neglect of efficient control and supervision of production matters. Suppliers of controlled price goods may resent the profits their client enterprises make which they consider to be at their expense.

It was against this kind of socio-economic background that the Chinese government introduced a series of reform measures, focused on the enterprise. The object was to transform a rather rigid bureaucratic organisation responding only to directives and instructions from higher authorities to an efficient and responsive production unit with powers of dynamic self-development. As China's experts saw it, to achieve this objective a number of steps had to be taken. The state no longer appropriated the whole profit of the enterprise but levied a corporation profit tax. In this way, profits became an important measure of enterprise success and the retention of profits gave the enterprise an incentive to work better for larger profits. At the same time, the controls exercised by the ministry or state organ in charge were considerably loosened so as to give the enterprise more autonomy. The number of products subject to planned allocation and price control was considerably reduced. By 1986, in the country as a whole, the number of products under the state plan had dropped from 120 kinds to 60 kinds. The means of production controlled by the State General Bureau of Materials and Equipment dropped from 253 kinds to 23. Even for such products, enterprises concerned could sell any surplus over allotted quota at negotiated or free prices. Profits retained might be used for specified purposes — reinvestment, welfare funds, bonus distribution, etc.

While trying to improve the external environment, the Chinese leaders have not neglected the reforms concerning the structure of state enterprises. The authoritative definition of state policy on this is given in a document issued by the Party's Central Committee in 1984 called "The Decision on the Reform of the Economic Structure". In 1987, the State Council issued three sets of regulations to give legislative effect to the Central Committee's 1984 decisions. Among the issues dealt with, the regulations demarcated the line of responsibility between professional managers and the Party Committee. In this way, the ambiguous relationship, a hindrance to efficient management, was clarified and managers could feel greater confidence in the authority they could exercise.

In addition to structural reforms, there was another urgent matter and it concerned outdated machinery and equipment used. The Chinese experts saw that the solution lay in three directions. The immediate task was to re-equip factories and enterprises with modern machinery purchased from abroad or to buy the know-how to make such machinery by licensing agreements. The second was to improve China's own capabilities to produce better designed machinery, equipment and products. The third was to invite foreign enterprises to start businesses in China. Each of these lines of action has their special difficulties.

Buying new equipment or know-how brings immediate and substantial benefits. The difficulty is that such purchases are expensive and have to be paid for in hard currency. Increasing exports of goods and services to expand hard currency earnings became a critical policy objective. According to Chinese customs statistics, China's exports increased in value from US$9.7 billion in 1978 to US$30.9 billion in 1986.

Based on contracts for importing technology and equipment examined and approved by the Ministry of Foreign Economic Relations and Trade, China signed 1,397 importing contracts amounting to US$4.95 billion from 1981 to 1985. Of this total, the imports of complete sets of machinery and key equipment accounted for 604 contracts totaling US$3.38 billion in value. In 1985 alone, 671 contracts were signed with a total contractual value of US$2.96 billion, of which 295 contracts amounting to US$2.23 billion involved the imports of complete sets of machinery and key equipment.

While using better designed equipment brings immediate benefits to enterprises, it is not feasible for a large country like China to depend on imported technology all the time. She must acquire capability to develop advanced technology on her own. One reason why China has lagged behind can be traced to the separation of Research and Development (R&D) from production. In industrial countries, there is an organic link between the two. Major industrial enterprises have their own R&D laboratories and workshops financed by their revenues and manned by their employees. In China, the separation of R&D from production was a consequence of adopting the Russian system. One of the major items in the reform programme relates to the restructuring of the R&D institutes. They can no longer depend entirely on the state budget for their income and have to depend increasingly on R&D contracts concluded with industrial enterprises. A consequence of this policy is the promulgation of patent laws and related matters.

The third arm of policy, foreign investment, has obvious advantages. Foreign investors bring to China not only advanced technology but also hard currency and modern management systems. All these are therefore welcome. There are, as usual, numerous attendant problems. When the reforms started in 1979, few Chinese officials had much knowledge of how foreign enterprises operated, infrastructure was not well developed, and business laws were non-existent. The Chinese system of employment was the opposite of the free labour market foreign businessmen knew. These and other matters meant that special arrangements had to be made to meet the needs of foreign investors.

Since 1979, China has made great exertions to improve the investment climate. More than 200 economic laws and regulations have been promulgated by the State Council and a quarter of these relate to foreign investment and foreign trade. Four Special Economic Zones and 15 coastal cities have been designated to receive foreign investors where they can enjoy a wide range of preferential treatment.

Despite her foreign exchange constraints, China has managed to find means to allow foreign investors, who bring in advanced technology, access to her domestic markets. Those without export performance could accumulate renminbi balances and these might be used to exchange for hard currency from other foreign firms with surplus of foreign currency and a shortage of renminbi. The others would apply to joint venture firms with export performance. Sales in the domestic market could be geared to export sales and, in this way, no difficulty would be experienced in remittance of profits or purchase of imported components. Thus, the earning of foreign exchange is not a paramount policy objective. The main benefits are seen as the introduction of advanced technology and acquaintance with modern management systems.

Foreign investment occupies a prominent place in the overall policy framework, being one of the three policy initiatives taken to revitalise China's enterprises. The other two are the re-equipping of her factories, communications industries and infrastructure with imported plant and equipment and the reorganisation of her research institutes. Despite the late start, the initial lack of experience and the many problems still remaining, China had been remarkably successful in attracting foreign investment. Up till the middle of 1987, more than 8,000 contracts with foreign investors have been signed and approved, representing an investment of more than US$17 billion, quite a substantial performance for nine years.

Now, what about the future? We get a clearer idea if we see foreign investment in the broad context of China's economic reforms. That is to say, what motivates the leaders to embark upon them and what the final outcome is expected to be. The objective has been clearly stated in the Central Committee's 1984 decision. From these reforms there will eventually emerge "a planned commodity economy based on public ownership". By "commodity economy", it is meant a system under which production is determined by prices and costs as fixed by market conditions. A planned commodity economy means that market conditions will not be the sole determinant except for certain farm products, minor articles of daily use and some service and repair businesses. The planning mechanism will be retained but will use economic levers such as monetary and fiscal policies rather than administrative control in detail.

The decision of the Central Committee then goes on to state: "The full development of a commodity economy is an indisputable stage in the economic growth of society and a prerequisite for our economic modernisation. It is the only way to invigorate out economy and prompt enterprises to raise their efficiency, carry out flexible operations and promptly adapt themselves to complex and changing social demands. This cannot be achieved by relying only on administrative means and mandatory plans." This is a clear authoritative statement of China's economic policy objectives. The many separate measures taken in so many different fields make sense only in this context.

On the question of how far China is from this objective of the full development of a commodity economy, a solid beginning has been made but a long journey lies ahead.

The difficulties to cope with are many, including multiple pricing, multiple sourcing of materials, a mixture of traditional and modern practices in their enterprise management system. Particularly troublesome is the wage and employment system which results in very low mobility of workers and staffs. Under such conditions, economic management at both the macro and micro levels face greater difficulties than that in a centrally directed system. Take the macro position, and major policy initiative must take into account possible inflationary implications. Given the differences of perception from different economic interests, or even persons with different temperaments, the emergence of concensus would not come easily.

Going back to the *status quo* would be unpopular with the public. Their living standards, range of choices and opportunities for improvement are visibly superior to what they were in 1978. The only realistic choice is to press ahead towards their objective as defined in the 1984 Central Committee Decision.

What we are seeing in China today is the final phase of the historical process of transforming an ancient civilisation into a modern industrial state. Just as Meiji Japan did 120 years ago, China has decided to come to terms with the modern world of science and technology, of business management and information systems. In the process of modernising, she offers some unique opportunities to foreign investors who understand her policy objectives and who take a long-term view of their investment.

2

America Looks at China
Part I — After Deng, What?*

Editors' Note (for Chapters 2 to 5)

During the Cold War, the Joint Economic Committee of the US Congress regularly held open hearings of what was happening in "Communist China" by leading US China experts ("China watchers") from both the academia and various government sectors, covering all important aspects of China's development: politics, economics, social development, population, international relations, military affairs and so on. These experts would submit their studies first before they were subsequently put together and published by the US Government Printing Office as a compendium of useful information on China.

In the days when China was closed to all foreign scholars and researchers, China experts in America were arguably the best informed interpreters of developments in China. Even through the 1980s, when economic reform and the open-door policy were initiated, China was still not fully open to foreign researchers. Partly because of this and partly because of the massive data and information based on China that the US government had built up during the Cold War period, America's China specialists had the best knowledge of and often held the most authoritative views on China's developments.

On 17 April 1991, the Joint Economic Committee assembled the study papers and published two volumes titled, China's Economic Dilemmas in the 1990s: The Problems of Reforms, Modernization, and Interdependence. China

---

*Published by IEAP as *IEAP Discussion Paper N0. 8* on 6 September 1991. This article and the following three were from a series of reviews on the study of China commissioned by the Joint Economic Committee of the US Congress. Some 60 experts, including world authorities on their subjects, contributed to this study.

was then still reeling from the shock of the Tiananmen incident in June 1989, and had just published its Eighth Five-Year Plan (1991 to 1995) and was very cautious about China's future course of reform and development.

The post-Tiananmen Chinese leadership was in fact sharply divided between not just the pro-reform and anti-reform camps, but more importantly, between those who favoured a slower pace of reform and those who wanted to resume the past reform momentum towards a market system. The political debate was centred on the relative merits of capitalism and socialism ("Mr. Capitalist vs. Mr. Socialist"). What the half-reformed Chinese economy became was a matter of great concern to the people both inside and outside of China.

Specifically for Western China experts, they were deeply worried if the Tiananmen affair could have derailed or at least seriously slowed the process of economic liberalisation and market reform, as clearly reflected in the aforementioned title of the two volumes. Deng Xiaoping was then 88 years old, and American scholars were also looking at the longer-term issue of China's potentially uncertain transition to the post-Deng era.

Goh Keng Swee understandably read these two volumes with great interest. He discussed the main problems and issues under four headings: (1) After Deng, What? (2) The Future of Reforms; (3) Absorbing Modern Technology; and (4) Correcting Systemic Weaknesses. He then organised his comments into four short readable papers and sent them to the Singapore government (Cabinet ministers and permanent secretaries) as IEAP Discussion Papers 8 to 11.

Goh started off by highlighting the inherent tension between the emphasis on morality or values and real politik or national interest in America's foreign policy discourse. That was particularly the case in the immediate aftermath of the Tiananmen incident as many American legislators and scholars were outraged by the violent crackdown. Today, America's foreign policy towards China is still underpinned by such tension, i.e. how to balance American advocacy of human rights and their real national interests.

The American scholars then were basically not concerned about "After Deng, Who?", as Deng had already appointed Jiang Zemin as successor. But they all saw a big challenge to China from "After Deng, What?". Some American scholars were very pessimistic about post-Deng China, taking the cue from the collapse of the Soviet Union and Eastern Europe. But Goh went along with the more hopeful views of David Lampton and Kenneth Liberthal, who argued that China would muddle through because of its fear of chaos (pa luan).

On the "Future of Reforms", It may be stressed that neither the American experts who were still obsessed with the Tiananmen affair, nor Goh, writing in September 1991, would have predicted that in February 1992 Deng would undertake his historic tour of Shenzhen (Nanxun) and decided to open up China for a more thorough-going market reform, thereby unleashing three decades of high economic growth and prosperity for China.

Thus, American scholars were discussing the problems of the half-reformed mixed economy like inflation and rent-seeking activities under the dual-price system; Chen Yun's solution by putting forth his version of restricted market reform based on the "Bird Cage" theory; the lack of independent commercial banking; the soft budget constraint for all SOEs (state-owned enterprises); and the bureaucratic management of enterprises and so on.

More up-to-date than the American scholars, Goh noted that the Seventh Party Plenum in December 1990 had put forth more reform-oriented proposals to remedy some of the problems that were discussed by American scholars. Goh nonetheless went along with the American scholars and lamented how China's ideologically based political system at that time, in bringing about stability, had also frustrated many well-intentioned efforts to increase efficiency through the market. Those problems had in fact lasted most of the 1990s.

Goh's views on China's ability to innovate and absorb modern technology were mixed. On the one hand, China could mobilise its technological resources to achieve some high-profile projects like nuclear weapons, missiles and satellite launching. On the other hand, its government-directed R&D efforts and lack of free enterprise system were not conducive to innovation and commercial application. But American scholars, as pointed out by Goh, were generally not aware that the more market-oriented township and village enterprises (TVEs) were doing better in technology upgrading.

On "Correcting Systemic Weaknesses", American scholars highlighted all kinds of problems and inefficiencies under China's half-reformed economy, particularly the existence of SOEs, which were each a community by itself with its "Iron Rice Bowl" work system, rather than an efficient production unit. On account of the centralisation of power in a Leninist-type Party, economic decisions were often based on political considerations, and that made it less rational and more difficult to predict. China's problems were also aggravated by the historically unclear relationship between the central and the localities.

In short, the divergent views of American scholars over the future course of China at that time was mainly caused by the great uncertainty in the aftermath of the Tiananmen Incident, as the Chinese leadership was also *divided among the ideologues and reformers. China would do all it can to avoid the kind of collapse in the Soviet Union, but that would leave China with a trade-off between ideology and economic progress. Goh took the view that "managing the trade-off will be less troublesome when the Long March generation leaves the scene".*

It appears as a historical irony that neither the American scholars nor Goh at that time had anticipated that Deng Xiaoping as the last of the Long March generation would soon boldly and brilliantly break China's dilemma of ideology and reform by undertaking the Nanxun and launching his "socialist market economy".

Not many Singaporeans are aware of the efficient way the US Congress keeps itself informed of world affairs. The Library of Congress is probably the largest and best-managed general library in the world. It contains 88 million items, including 26 million books and pamphlets, with 1.4 million volumes in Chinese, Japanese, and other Asian languages. The library's holding of manuscripts and other archive material, photographs, sound recordings, films and maps runs to tens of millions of items.

The numerous Committees of Congress keep themselves informed by commissioning special studies in their areas of interest. In such undertakings, the Library of Congress has at its disposal the whole range of top-ranking experts in American universities and think-tanks. Not unnaturally, the studies are both authoritative and readable. Singaporeans who do not have the time or inclination to plod through books and academic journals but want a short cut to information on a subject of interest could profitably consult the Congressional Research Service's publications.

In April 1991, in response to a request by the Joint Economic Committee of Congress, the Research Service produced a study entitled "China's Economic Dilemmas in the 1990s: The Problems of Reforms, Modernization and Interdependence". This two-volume study comprised more than 60 papers. In this series of studies, I will review the papers dealing with subjects likely to interest well-informed Singaporeans.

The papers were written with the memory of the Tiananmen tragedy fresh in the authors' minds. This has left a clear mark on most of the papers. We are thereby repeatedly reminded of the propensity of Americans to pass moral judgements. As one of the authors said, "American people, media, interest groups and, to a considerable degree, US legislators place a strong emphasis on morality or values as well as real politic or national interest in American foreign policy."[1]

Expressions of moral outrage were most evident in Carol Lee Hamrin's "The Economic Costs of Intellectual Alienation". According to her, the Tiananmen Incident had resulted in a "fundamental loss of legitimacy of the Chinese Communist Party among the educated elite and informed urban populace". People had lost confidence that the Party could make China rich, strong and internationally respected.[2]

Other writers, while condemning the use of firepower on unarmed citizens, devoted more attention to basic political and economic issues. The clearest answer to the question of what happens after Deng's departure comes from Christopher M. Clarke, an Intelligence Research Specialist at the State Department.[3] After Deng, he expects Yang Shangkun to take over the leadership, but Yang has to share this with other elders — Chen Yun, Peng Zhen, Wang Zhen and others.

Clarke does not expect this group leadership to be effective in finding answers to the country's difficulties. They will not respond to calls for democracy in a spirit of conciliation, nor will they offer new solutions to the pressing problems of the day. Slogans and not creative innovation will be the responses on offer. Economic policy will move in the direction of strengthening central policy. The egalitarian policies of the past will find favour. Dissent will be countered with control, coercion and repression.

---

[1] Robert G. Sutter, "External Factors Affecting the Economy", in Joint Economic Committee, Congress of the US, *China's Economic Dilemmas in the 1990s: The Problems of Reforms, Modernization and Interdependence* (Washington DC, US Govt Printing Office 1991), Vol. 1, pp. 48–64.

[2] Carol Lee Hamrin, "The Economic Costs of Intellectual Alienation" in Joint Economic Committee, Congress of the US, *op. cit.*, pp. 308–320.

[3] Christopher M. Clarke, "China's Transition to the Post-Deng Era", in Joint Economic Committee, Congress of the US, *op. cit.*, pp. 1–14.

Clarke expects that this post-Deng leadership will resemble that of Leonid Brezhnev in the Soviet Union. The state apparatus will be dominated by younger hardliners and the outcome will be Brezhnev-style stagnation. There will be no transition to a Western-style multi-party political structure because China lacks the "historical, cultural and socio-economic" background necessary to affect this transition.

However, Clarke believes that China will not revert to the Maoist anarchy of past decades. The experience of fast growth in the 1980s and memories of the chaos of the Cultural Revolution effectively shut out this option. But the post-Deng leadership will not be able to accomplish the substantial potential the Chinese economy has for improvements in efficiency; nor can it restore the impressive growth rates of the reform decade.

That decade had created "rising expectations". Influenced by knowledge of the outside world, China's population will be "harder to lead, less forgiving of leadership mistakes, and less willing to accept slogans in place of performance". The cause of this gloomy prediction can be traced to Clarke's assessment of the political system. There does not exist any set procedures in leadership appointments by way of "entry, exit or popular evaluation" as practised in Western-type democratic systems. This explains the backroom internecine strife among leaders. This prevents effective government and erodes public support.

Kenneth Lieberthal, of Michigan University, carries Clarke's analysis a step further.[4] The Leninist party structure in general adoption in socialist states possesses special features not found elsewhere. These include effective control of information, an ability to coerce people and a unique system of mass mobilisation to achieve the leadership's political objectives.

Some changes were made to this structure in the 1980s. For instance, decentralisation of authority to provinces has reduced the risk of committing egregious folly such as the Cultural Revolution and the Great Leap Forward. Nevertheless, the essential Leninist

---

[4] Kenneth Liberthal, "The Dynamics of Internal Policies", in Joint Economic Committee, Congress of the US, *op. cit.*, pp. 15–28.

features remain. Because of Party controls, information flows are poor as compared with market economies. The top–down command system encourages information flows along vertical lines. That is, a ministry communicates easily with departments and units under its control. But information exchanges between ministries and co-operation along horizontal lines, i.e. between units of the same rank but answering to different ministries, become difficult to manage.

In today's electronic age of business management nourished by instant flows of information, the Chinese system places their enterprises at a severe disadvantage. In the early decades of communist rule, the Chinese system could produce extensive progress because of its strength in the mobilisation of people and resources in building railways, roads, steel works, iron and coal mines. That age of extensive development has been superceded by technology-intensive industries. These flourish only when information flows freely.

Singapore investors in China can testify to the validity of Liberthal's criticism. Getting information presents difficulties which these investors have not experienced in other countries. Kenneth Liberthal sees more serious dangers than frustrations of prospective foreign investors. When making decisions on matters of political significance, the system easily loses contact with reality. Political issues, unlike economic variables, are difficult to quantify and judgement involves a significantly subjective element.

Such a reporting arrangement encourages the upward flow of information which is designed to please superiors. The expression of contrary views seldom takes place because of the real or perceived risks involved. Where information is useful, as often happens with business information, Liberthal notes that this is usually hoarded as a business asset to be parted with only in exchange for something of equivalent value.

The outcome, according to him, can result in defective co-ordination among ministries/departments as co-ordinators work on flawed data. Yet the inferior outcome may not be revealed because of the secrecy surrounding information flows.

How, then, would the post-Deng leaders cope with the increasing difficulties in store for them? Will there be a break-up of the system as we are now witnessing in the Soviet Union and Eastern Europe? There are so many parallels that such an outcome cannot be considered fanciful. Yet none of the American scholars expect this to happen, not even the outraged Miss Hamrin.

This hopeful prediction is best argued by David Lampton, President of the National Committee on US–China Relations.[5] He states that it is a mistake to believe that China is a political and social volcano waiting to erupt in the next few years. It is true that the country faces a frightening catalogue of troubles. These he listed as chronic budget deficits, danger of inflation, diminished legitimacy of the leaders, massive unemployment and underemployment, alienation of intellectuals, rising expectations, inefficient state enterprises, huge government subsidies, loss of central government power relative to the provinces and uncertainty over leadership succession.

On top of all these problems, the leaders cannot agree on how to manage the transition to a more market-oriented economy. But Lampton makes the point that the queues and scarcities which pressed consumers beyond endurance in Eastern Europe and the Soviet Union are not seen in China's major cities. "Life may not be great," he said, "but it is literally light years ahead of what has catalyzed the breakdown in the Soviet Union and fostered disturbances in Central Europe."

Lampton rests his hopes on more than enough supplies of consumer goods. He reminds readers that Chinese society is predominantly comprised of peasants. Chinese peasants live differently from the urban society of the West or of China, for that matter. They are not well educated and still retain many of China's traditional beliefs and customs. The reform decade had brought them a steady increase in living standards.

Evidence of this improvement can be seen in the burgeoning rural markets, the proliferation of new peasant homes visible from roads and railways and, most noteworthy, the explosion of rural industries in newly built townships. The rural population provides the sheet anchor

---

[5] David M. Lampton, "China's Biggest Problem: Gridlock, Not Revolution", in Joint Economic Committee, Congress of the US, *op. cit.*, pp. 65–69.

of political stability. Throughout China's long history, the overthrow of dynastic rule occurred only after prolonged and intense peasant unrest.

As for the urban workers, Lampton notes a strange irony in their situation. The very inefficiency of state enterprises has produced a contented labour force. They cannot be dismissed; they live in virtually rent-free enterprise houses, and they enjoy subsidized medical treatment, free education for their children and other welfare benefits. A worker's average pay is higher than that of a newly recruited graduate engineer; the demands their employer makes on them during working hours are reasonable. The worker has become a conservative force, preferring the security of a planned economy to the uncertainties of the market economy.

Lampton neatly sums up the tragedy of the Chinese intellectuals after the Tiananmen Incident. "The dreams of China's intellectuals seem not to be the dreams of China's peasants and workers." As a consequence, conditions making for widespread protest and social upheaval remain weak, apart from the alienated intellectuals. Since the monopoly of power remains with the Communist Party, these intellectuals cannot propagate their views in any useful public platform. Nor could one expect widespread clamour for equal chances for all parties to present their case for the public to judge. This reason is peculiarly Chinese.

All American scholars note that the fear of chaos (in Chinese *luan*) forms a deeply ingrained sentiment among Chinese people. No doubt, educated Chinese have historic memories of the chaos into which the country was plunged since the Opium Wars of the 19th century followed by numerous rebellions, the fall of the Qing dynasty and further chaos created by the warlords and the Japanese invasion. Another piece of irony in recent history is that Mao's visionary Great Leap Forward and Cultural Revolution have convinced the Chinese people by first-hand experience that chaos is not a remote historical experience. These events had been preceded by much public debate in which differing views were expressed. As such, a repeat performance holds little attraction.

Kenneth Liberthal supports Clarke's views on Chinese fear of chaos in contributing to stability. He believes that whichever way the leadership succession works out, those engaged in the struggle will preserve an outward appearance of calm and will try to conceal their differences from public gaze. The alternative would be a sizeable risk of disorder. His final judgement is that despite the various known weaknesses, the political apparatus remains extremely powerful with a network of party cadres and security personnel of enormous size. Hence the consensus among American scholars is that the rule of the Communist Party in China is as secure as any human institution can be in a fast-changing world.

A subject of interest to several scholars concerns the effectiveness of pressures of the international community on China. Clarke believes that the goodwill enjoyed by China before the Tiananmen Incident has been lost and is unlikely to be regained soon. Western support on issues such as General Agreement on Tarrifs and Trade (GATT) assessment will be uncertain. Trade frictions will increase.

Robert G Sutter, Senior Specialist at the Congressional Research. Service, believes that foreign pressures will not produce significant changes in China's policy. Despite intense pressure in 1989 and 1990, China's leaders did not significantly alter the course of foreign policy. He attributes their ability to absorb foreign pressures to several factors.

First, the leaders, both hardliners and reformists, agree that the open door policy must continue for the sake of economic progress. Next, countries in East Asia, especially Japan, have made it clear that they have no intention to isolate China, despite the sanctions imposed. The fact of leadership division means that any major change of domestic or foreign policy as a response to foreign pressures would be difficult to gain consensus. If one takes into account the impending succession of leaders from one generation to the next, none of the contending leaders wish to be judged soft.

What American scholars did not mention is the limited impact of economic sanctions on economic growth. The withholding of loans, discouragement of investments and tourists have made little impact on general living standards. The economic difficulties experienced by the Chinese are of their own making and the remedies lie in their hands and not those of foreigners. Foreign direct investment and foreign loans would make their tasks less painful but, in themselves, will not solve the country's troubles. The solution lies in advancing economic reforms along lines that would increase prosperity without producing a crisis of inflation, corruption and privileged wealth that brought about the troubles of 1989.

Goh Keng Swee
2 September 1991

3

America Looks at China
Part II — Future of Reforms

Harry Harding, Senior Fellow, Foreign Policy Studies Programme of the Brookings Institution, asks why the future of China's economic reforms is important.[1] Harding states "China's economic productivity, rate of growth and standards of living will be determined by the fate of its economic reforms."

As of now, he finds several reasons to believe that this fate hangs in the balance. Some of the reasons are based on recent events. They can be traced to responses to the serious problems created in 1988 by reform programmes — inflation, corruption and the emergence of high living among a privileged minority. These created widespread resentment among the urban intellectuals dependent on fixed salaries.

As a counter-measure, the central authorities embarked on an anti-inflationary programme in the autumn of 1988. This effort was further strengthened by policy measures described in detail in a document issued by the Party's Central Committee in November 1989, sometimes referred to as the "Central Committee's Decision

---

*Published by IAEP as *IEAP Discussion Paper No. 9* on 13 September 1991.
[1] Harry Harding, "The Problematic Future of China's Economic Reforms", in Joint Economic Committee, Congress of the US. *China's Economic Dilemmas in the 1990s: The Problems of Reforms, Modernization, and Interdependence* (Washington DC, US Govt Printing Office, 1991), Vol. 1. pp. 78–88.

on Economic Policy". The Decision, according to Harding, correctly diagnosed some causes. For instance, during 1988–89 inflation was caused by excessive expansion of note issue and bank credit. A major. cause of corruption was the large gap between low administered prices and high market prices. This provided opportunities for corruption to those in charge of releasing commodities at administered prices, as buyers were willing to offer bribes.

Some of the anti-inflationary measures were rational, such as credit tightening and reduction of state capital expenditure. In other areas, policy measures represented a reversal of reforms. Price control was introduced extensively. Mandatory state controls over commodity allocations increased (whereas previous policy was to reduce them). Central licensing of imports and exports was re-introduced. Central control over bank credit was reinforced by direct administrative measures.

Another retrograde step took the form of increasing the authority of the Party branch in enterprise decision-making. Previously most professional managers of state enterprises enjoyed full authority in day-to-day operations and the Party officials attended to matters such as political education of employees. Perhaps the most damaging impact the Decision had on reforms was to place large- and medium-sized state enterprises in a favoured position in respect of supplies of raw materials, components, energy, transportation and bank credit at the expense of other enterprises. The township enterprises — set up by township authorities in charge of a group of villages — were singled out for tough treatment and deprived of free access to these supplies.

These measures indicated a substantial reduction of support of the present leaders of economic reform to liberalise the economy. Harding found an anti-reform bias in discussions in China's papers and journals. Excessive dependence on the markets became a target of attack as did thorough-going privatisation. Articles extolling the role of mandatory planning, insisting on the primacy of public ownership, previously rare, became more frequent.

Not surprisingly, the climate of discussion was not as lively and open as before June 1989. The disbanding of the Party's Rural Development Research Centre and the State Council's Institute for Economic System Reforms and the closure of Shanghai's World

Economic Herald weakened the position of reformist intellectuals. To sum up, mainstream expert opinion favoured Chen Yun's "Restricted Bird Cage".

When reforms ran into trouble, the change in the climate of official opinion as described by Harding could be taken as a natural consequence. The question arises whether this change represents a temporary swing of the pendulum or a durable shift of policy. The latter cannot be ruled out.

Harding believes that further attempts to liberalise the economy by strengthening market forces will challenge the interests of powerful groups in Chinese society. He explains this in terms of specific reform items — price reform, enterprise management reform and financial reform.

Because prices of administered goods had been set very low, price reform must mean raising prices to higher levels, eventually to international levels for tradeable goods. The unavoidable result is cost-push inflation of substantial dimension. Many of these prices relate to politically sensitive items such as staple foods, housing, transport and utilities. There will be built-in resistance to the full implementation of price reforms.

Enterprise management reforms, in relation to state enterprises, really centre on the removal of "soft budget constraints". China's state enterprises, in line with state enterprises in other socialist countries, do not fear incurring losses. Losses can be attributed to low prices fixed for their output and the unwillingness of authorities to approve higher prices. In any event, losses are made good by state subsidies — hence the name "soft budget constraint".

Hardening the budget constraint as practised by capitalist enterprises would lead to widespread bankruptcies and extensive unemployment. Even before these occur, enterprise managers will introduce cost-cutting measures, enforce discipline in the work force and raise quality. All these will be opposed by local labour officials concerned with preserving labour peace, by trade unions and even by enterprise managers who will find the new system very trying on their nerves.

One item of financial reform relates to the erosion of control over state revenues from the centre to the provinces, cities and local authorities caused by decentralisation of authority. Naturally, any effort to reverse the distribution of revenue will be strongly resisted by provinces, cities and localities. There is another item of financial reform which has received scant notice in the literature and that is the reform of China's banking system. It is here that the ultimate source of instability can be traced. But the lack of information from Chinese official sources has created an area of ignorance on the subject.

Resistance to further reforms, observes Harding, is thus built into the system. It will take an exceptionally daring leadership to break down such resistance. So Harding contemplates an alternative to pushing reforms ahead, and that is for China to settle for slower growth and lower efficiency. He quoted a Chinese intellectual's view that a sustained growth rate of 3% a year might, by reducing the demand for reform, pose the greatest threat to China's reformists. Harding captures this sentiment by reversing Voltaire's epigram, "The good may be the enemy of the best." In a future instalment, I shall argue that this comfortable option is not available to China.

Robert F. Dernberger, Professor of Economics University of Michigan, assesses the current stage of China's economy reached after the reform decade.[2] It can be described as a "mixed economic system" in which markets and central plans co-exist. This mixture has weakened the principal function of markets. This function is for market prices to send signals to producers and consumers, so that they make rational decisions as to what to buy, produce and sell.

Where market prices reflect relative scarcities and costs, price signals would co-ordinate producer and consumer effectively. Resources are then used to the best advantage to get supply to meet demand. But prices in a mixed economy are often negotiated prices reached under the eye of a supervising authority. Dernberger observes that markets become "grey markets". Competition exists mainly on the buyer side. The supply side, especially for raw materials, is dominated by central or provincial authorities who retain powers to allocate a percentage of these.

---

[2] Robert F. Dernberger, "China's Mixed Economic System — Properties and Consequences", in Joint Economic Committee, Congress of the US, *op. cit.*, pp. 89–101.

The exercise of political authority is clearly seen in the banking system and the market for loans. The allocation of the most important factor of production — loan capital — is thus determined not by the market but by state agencies. Commercial banks do not operate as independent enterprises motivated by the desire to put the country's savings to the most profitable uses. The absence of a capital market has meant that decisions on loan allocations are made on political, not business, grounds.

Dernberger shares Harding's opinion that the present leaders will not push hard for reforms. In brief, he thinks the favoured "mixed economy" will have the following elements. First, dominant central control will remain in place. Second, the planned system will allocate "key commodities" — raw materials, semi-finished goods, transportation, utilities — and the market sector will be subject to administrative constraints. Third, the "soft-budget constraint" will remain, that is state enterprises will continue to have their losses made good out of the state budget.

Dernberger believes China's leaders do not have the political will to push reforms to the stage where the market gives proper signals to enterprises, buyers and sellers. In some of his footnotes, he makes some interesting revelations of the private thinking of China's leaders and top bureaucrats. Former Vice-Premier Yao Yilin told him that China's economic reforms will be completed some time in the middle of the 21st century. As regards hardening the soft budget constraints, State Planning Commission officials expressed opinions such as "that would lead to unemployment" or "that would have a negative impact on the budget" or "the workers wouldn't accept that".

Dernberger makes a powerful point about the various forms of enterprise ownership. In scholarly Chinese journals, articles discuss the merits and demerits of different forms of ownership — state, co-operative, private, individual. But this discussion has paid insufficient attention to the rights of ownership. Ownership implies the right to sell or transfer property owned, and sell the output of goods and services and receive income in return. This means that there should be well defined property rights and a legal system to enforce them. The present situation is ambiguous on important issues, thereby creating opportunities for arbitrary interference by even low level bureaucrats.

Another reform expert, Dwight Perkins of the Harvard Institute for International Development, concentrates on two items of the reform programme — price reform and reform of managements of state enterprises.[3] His views on price reform and the functions of market prices are similar to Dernberger's.

It is in the behaviour of enterprise managers that China differs most markedly from that seen in competitive market economies. We are accustomed to expect enterprise managers to maximise profits or market share. Either way, they strive to cut costs, improve quality and increase sales. They do not lobby political leaders for state subsidies, negotiate for special tax treatment or ask for monopoly rights.

Enterprise managers in China (and other socialist countries) do not behave in accordance with "market rules" as described earlier. In pre-reform years, enterprise managers aim to maximise the gross value of output, that is, they try to meet the output targets assigned to them from above and exceed them if possible. To do this, they need to hoard raw materials, as supplies of these are not dependable.

After the reforms, managers do try to maximise profits as their pay and bonuses and those of other employees are linked to profits. However, because of incomplete price reforms, profit maximisation does not result in the same behaviour observed in market economies, i.e. reduce costs, improve quality, etc. Profits may be increased by negotiating with superior authorities for lower tax rates, greater freedom to sell output in the open market, greater supplies of price-controlled raw materials and bigger loans at subsidised interest rates. A greater premium gets placed on negotiating skills, political clout or "*guanxi*" in Chinese, than on efficient management as understood in market economies.

Whereas, in China, the Central Bank lacks independence due to political pressure, Perkins notes that the system has a built-in

---

[3] Dwight H. Perkins, "Markets versus Plans: The Key Role of Enterprise Manager Behavior?", in Joint Economic Committee, Congress of the US, *op. cit.*, pp. 160–166.

inflationary bias. Credit will be expanded to increase output in accordance with the desires of central or provincial authorities. This, together with the successful outcome of enterprise negotiation with superior authorities to raise prices of output, will increase profits substantially during a business upswing. Wages and bonuses will also increase, thereby adding a demand-pull impetus to the original cost push.

Inflation strengthens the political call to slow down and even reverse price reforms and this, in turn, strengthens the power of superior authorities over enterprise managers. Managers will then be less inclined to go by market rules. Perkins concludes that freeing prices by reducing the area of negotiations between enterprises and authorities will help the behaviour of managers to react in accordance with market rules.

This is not easy to accomplish in China. Perkins believes that it is necessary to sever the ties between the enterprise and the bureaucracy. One way to achieve this is to create new forms of public ownership to cut the links between supervising authorities and enterprise management. The Central Bank must have independent powers and commercial banks must have the authority to extend loans on business, not political considerations.

The articles reviewed here suffer from one unavoidable disadvantage. They were written at various times in 1990. Information published this year was not available to the authors. In this way, they became unduly influenced by the Decision of the Central Committee of November 1989. The conclusions of this document bore all the hallmarks of hardline ideologues, such as re-centralisation of authority, increased power to the State Planning Commission, reversal of price reforms, favoured treatment of state enterprises, denial of resources to township enterprises and administrative control over credit supplies.

It is reasonable to infer from the Central Committee document that the Chinese leaders were reluctant to press ahead with reforms. However, the damaging effect of the Decision's policies on China's economic and financial performance in 1990 had two results. First, another top-level policy re-assessment took place, and second, the prestige of the ideologues declined.

While the Decision succeeded in reducing inflation to around 2.1% in 1990, it created other problems. Foremost among these was the increase in the budget deficit which the Decision had expected to decline. Subsidies to state enterprises doubled in 1990 as compared to 1989. Price subsidies reached the level where they exceeded the defence budget.

These results were reported by Finance Minister Wang Bingquan in March 1991. In May, he raised the prices of wheat flour and rice by 70%, cooking oil by 150%. State Planning Minister Zou Jiahua announced, also in March 1991, a policy of reviving private enterprises in the trade and service industries to combat rising urban unemployment. He also recommended that measures be taken to prevent rural workers engaged in agriculture from changing their occupations without permission. This probably is the result of the Decision measures taken against township enterprises which employ rural people.

In December 1990, the Central Committee submitted proposals to the Seventh Plenary Session of the Party. These proposals were clearly reform-oriented. For instance, it mentioned the need for state enterprises to have genuine independent management. Township enterprises were deemed an important component of the national economy. Most significantly, it recommended pressing ahead on price reforms and limiting controls to a small number of goods and services. While these proposals re-affirm reform policies, they do not explain how the troubles which undermined reforms in 1988–1989 could be avoided once economic expansion gets going.

These recent developments do not impair the validity of the analysis of American scholars on basic issues. In fact, they highlight the dilemma China's leaders find themselves in. Marxist ideology fortifies the political system and gives it stability. But the three combined — ideology, system and stability — frustrate in a hundred and one ways and in thousands of places, any well-intentioned efforts to use the free market mechanism to raise economic efficiency. These articles explain the economic logic that has produced this outcome.

Goh Keng Swee
2 September 1991

4

America Looks at China
Part III — Absorbing Modern Technology*

China cannot be considered backward in the production of weapons sytems. She produces nuclear tipped missiles, operates a commercial satellite launching service and is building a fleet of nuclear powered submarines. Socialist countries have demonstrated that they do not lag behind capitalist states in weapons production. It is in production and distribution of civilian goods, things that raise living standards, that their performance shows major weaknesses.

When assessing China's performance, we should keep a sense of proportion. We should note the wide range of goods they produce which Singapore does not, for instance, heavy duty trucks, buses, locomotives, small transport aircraft and a wide range of machinery and machine tools. Though these perform their functions adequately, China's problem is that the design for most of these are outdated and their technical performance usually does not reach world standards.

Denis Fred Simon, Associate Professor, Tufts University quoted a survey done in the mid-1980s on the condition of industrial

---

*Published by IEAP as *IEAP Discussion Paper No. 10* on 20 September 1991.

equipment.[1] 10%–20% were of pre-1950 vintage. Most, about 60%, belonged to the 1950–60 generation. The remainder, 20% to 25%, were fairly modern of 1970s–80s design. The estimate was that some 60% of equipment needed to be replaced. Such is the background to the need to upgrade its technology by installing more modern machinery. This need to upgrade technology has been fully understood by the authorities since the reforms began and technology upgrading occupies a central position in the government's economic policy.

Denis Simon reported a substantial response in this area. Between 1981–1991, Chinese official records show that more than 18,000 agreements were concluded to procure equipment and know-how for upgrading state enterprises. Total expenditure amounted to US$98.5 billion, including US$27 billion of imported equipment. Even by standards of a large country, this represents a massive effort. How did the authorities ensure that the money was well spent?

It is interesting to compare how decisions are made on technology upgrading in a planned system as compared with a free enterprise system. In the latter, decisions are made by enterprises based on their judgement of market trends, cost of loan capital, the state of competition and such like. In China, the mechanism is more complicated, as described by Denis Simon and another expert, Richard P. Suttmeier.[2]

The State Planning Commission lays down the priority areas for technology upgrading in successive Five-Year Plans (FYP). For instance, the Seventh FYP listed some 3,000 items of key equipment designated for purchase during 1986–88. The Eighth FYP defined priority areas in a different way. First, high technology useful in advancing research in high energy physics, micro-electronics, computer science, biotechnology, ocean engineering and materials science.

---

[1] Denis Fred Simon, "China's Acquisition and Assimilation of Foreign Technology: Beijing's Search for Excellence" in Joint Economic Committee, Congress of the US, *China's Economic Dilemmas in the 1990s: The Problems of Reforms, Modernization, and Interdependence*, Washington DC, US Govt Printing Office, 1991 Vol. 2, pp. 565–598.

[2] Richard P. Suttmeier, "China's High Technology: Programs, Problems and Prospects", in Joint Economic Committee, Congress of the US, *op. cit.*, pp. 544–564.

Second, technology which will improve China's production of energy, raw materials, agriculture and transportation facilities which are in chronically short supply. Third, technology and equipment needed to improve performance of export industries. Export industries provide the foreign exchange used in buying foreign equipment.

Actual implementation of priority projects takes on a number of forms. Special programmes, initiated by the Party or the State Council, assist in identifying state enterprises most likely to succeed. In 1986, the Party Central Committee approved the 863 programme based on a proposal submitted in March 1986 (hence the number 863) to Deng Xiaoping by laser specialist Wang Dahang and three other scientists. The 863 programme monitors domestic research in priority areas and identifies and assists those with promise of commercial applications.

Another programme, the Torch Plan, was launched in August 1988 by the State Science and Technology Commission of the State Council. It has established some thirty Service Centres throughout China to provide selected enterprises with assistance in finance, equipment purchase, marketing, taxes, foreign travel. Its role is to act as "technology incubators" assisting the transfer of technology from the laboratory to commercial production. During 1988–89, 272 projects (out of 1,500 applications) received assistance under the Torch Plan. All these projects fell within the priority areas defined in the Eighth FYP.

The state provides special incentives to selected enterprises in priority areas under the FYP. These include reduction in sales tax on output produced by imported foreign technology when such output replaces imports. In addition, those who buy the output will have to pay part of the purchase price in foreign currency. Where the equipment or components have to be imported because they are not produced in China, import duty may be reduced or waived. Selected enterprises enjoy preference in the allocation of foreign exchange, bank loans and supply of controlled materials. Finally, staff and workers of enterprises judged to have successfully absorbed and digested foreign technology receive special bonuses.

Suttmeier states that it is too early to pass judgment on the performance of 863 and Torch. There is little doubt that considerable effort and manpower resources have been mobilised in the programmes. In 1988, there were 5,275 state research institutes employing 384,000 scientists and engineers. In addition, there were 2,498 research institutes under local governments and a further 4,870 smaller collective and private research institutes. Tertiary education institutions — universities and polytechnics — numbered 1,063 and these engaged 161,000 staff in research and development (R&D). Suttmeier estimates that a total of 450,000 scientists and engineers were engaged in full-time R&D work in 1988. Total expenditure on such R&D projects amounted to US$2.5 billion.

Denis Simon was less inhibited than Suttmeier in passing judgement on China's performance. Possibly the field work he did in China, in the course of which he noted several blunders, warned him of the dangers of unfulfilled expectations.

Successful transplants of new technology depend critically on the ability of government officials to make right decisions. Denis Simon doubts their ability to do so because the way these decisions were made remain unclear. First, how do the authorities choose enterprises which are to get special access to loans and foreign exchange? Second, what is the proper level at which decisions should be made on technology upgrading? What criteria should be used in selecting appropriate technology, equipment and supplies?

We can see that in a market economy, enterprises (including commercial banks) make these decisions. They have to live with the results and hence collect reliable and comprehensive information to back their judgement. The track records of enterprises are public knowledge and technical consultants' services are available. By contrast, the restrictions on information flows in China act as a severe handicap to officials who have to make these critical decisions.

Roy F. Grow, Professor of Political Science Department, Carleton College, contributed an interesting account of how enterprises actually introduce technology.[3] For ten years, he had served as a

---

[3] Roy F. Grow, "In Search of Excellence in China's Industrial Sector: The Chinese Enterprise and Foreign Technology", in Joint Economic Committee, Congress of the US, *op. cit.*, pp. 817–827.

consultant for many American and Japanese companies who sold equipment to Chinese enterprises. During that period, he studied more than one hundred instances of technology transfers.

Whereas Simon and Suttmeier view technology absorption in terms of national policies and implementation programmes, Grow describes, through case studies, what takes palce where the action is — in the enterprise. This perspective is complementary to the other and improves our understanding of how the system works.

The manager of a component plant in Shenyang, faced with declining business, decided to acquire new die-cutting technology After prolonged discussions with other managers and officials, he invited an American and a Japanese firm to present proposals for upgrading the factory's heating furnace. This was only the first step of a long process.

First, the enterprise manager entered into a series of consultations with workers, engineers and trade unions. As the new production system would affect work assignments, work rules and job specifications, the acceptance of workers to these changes had to be secured. Engineers had to study the relative efficiency of the two proposals on offer.

The next stage concerned upstream enterprises, suppliers of steel and energy and their agreement to changes in supplies had to be obtained. Downstream enterprises — purchasers of the factory's output of components — had to be consulted about quality, prices and problems of down time during installation of new equipment.

Third, the agencies of government had to give their agreement. These included the Central Ministry of Metallurgical Industries, the China National Automotive Industry Corporation and various industry bureaus of the Liaoning Provincial Government. All parties in these three sets of consultations must signify at least their tacit agreement. In China, obtaining such clearances calls for negotiating skills, patience and plenty of leg work. In this instance, more than two years passed between the start of technical studies by the company's engineering staff and the signature of the contract with the foreign supplier — the American company.

Roy Grow believes that China's large state enterprises lack the initiative to introduce innovation because the task of obtaining agreements with their enormous work force, the large number of supervising authorities and upstream and downstream associates, would deter their managers from even making a start. There are too many conflicting group interests to be reconciled. Hence his conclusion that the heart of China's technology acquisition process is found in smaller enterprises whose managers possess entrepreneurial qualities. Under such leadership, enterprises become more agile, more sensitive to change and more able to effect change.

It is not difficult to resolve the apparent contradiction between Grow's account and the other two which describe technology acquisition by large state enterprises. There are some 40,000 state enterprises in China and Grow had contacts with only a tiny sample of them. So far as the large state enterprises go, all three scholars agree that initiative needs to be taken at high level in central ministries before new technology gets introduced.

This conclusion receives support from the fourth expert — Erik Baark, Associate Professor, Technical University of Denmark.[4] He gave an account of an interesting innovation introduced by the reformers in the mid-1980s. This is the establishment of "technology markets". Technology was deemed to consist of design, prototypes, or general know-how and were regarded as "commodities" available for sale and purchase. Sellers and buyers were domestic enterprises and institutes.

Transactions were conducted several ways. Technology shops were initially opened in Shenyang and Shanghai and spread to other cities. Technology trade fairs, permanent or travelling, did good business. Brokers emerged in 1985–86 and research also made direct contacts with customers.

The government encouraged trade in technology in several ways. The funding of research institutes from the state budget was reduced

---

[4] Erik Baark, "Fragmented Innovation: China's Science and Technology Policy Reforms in Retrospect", in Joint Economic Committee, Congress of the US, *op. cit.*, pp. 531–545.

to encourage them to earn income through technology sales. New laws such as the Patent Law of 1985 and the Technology Contract Law of 1987 helped to reduce fraudulent practices which had crept up, and to place transactions in technology transfers on a firmer basis.

Baark noted that large state enterprises were minor players in the burgeoning technology trade. During 1985–86, small enterprises, especially village and township enterprises, were the main customers, but in later years, medium-sized state enterprises showed increasing interest.

In the late 1980s, Beijing's "Electronic Street" in the Zhongguancun area made its appearance and registered sensational growth. The main participants were private companies manned by electronic and computer engineers, graduates of China's universities. Technology sales, both domestic and export, increased at an unprecedented rate. The star performer was the Stone Company whose head, Wan Runnan, came to grief over the Tiananmen Incident.

Baark believes that the Chinese bureaucracy hold mixed views on Electronics Street. The reformers of course welcomed the successes but the others did not. He states, "In addition to the academic contempt toward such commercial flair, which is a distinctive feature of both traditional Confucian values and more recent communist dogmatism, there was a fear of the political consequences of 'private' enterprises." Such conservative attitude will limit China's advances in technology, states Baark.

Suttmeier advances a more cogent reason for a pessimistic outlook. He argues that the vast system of research institutes as entities separate from enterprises has led to "the bottling of research results in laboratories". The underlying lesson seems to be that a high-technology strategy which is cut off from competition in a mass market is ultimately unsustainable without enormous government subsidies.

A competitive mass market is more than large numbers of consumers with money to spend. Consumers must have the right to spend as they think fit and producers must have genuine autonomy to use their resources to the best advantage. Ultimately, their right to behave in this way is a matter of individual rights and liberties that must be guaranteed by a modern legal system.

Suttmeier does not explain how the links operate between a competitive mass market and productive R&D and why both cannot work without a modern legal system. These issues go to the heart of China's economic difficulties. In the meantime, we should note supporting views of other scholars.

Roy Grow, with an extensive experience of China's business methods, recommends that basic changes are needed not only to enterprise management systems but also to laws on banking, financial institutions and accounting procedures. He quotes Chinese managers arguing for legislation in key areas as status of party officials in enterprises, inspection systems for maintaining quality control, methods of changing work assignments and procedures on dealing with work grievances. Ambiguities in these areas serve to dampen any innovative spirit which Chinese managers may have.

There is one area of technology transfer which scholars — American and others — have often overlooked. That comprises what the literature calls "township enterprises". The focus of attention centred on how state enterprises — large, medium or small — upgraded technology. Only Baark noted, and that merely in passing, that the largest buyers of technology in the newly established technology market were small-scale and rural enterprises, often called "township enterprises".

These are sited in townships serving a collection of villages, absorbing their surplus farm workers in new industrial enterprises. Such enterprises may be privately owned or they may be owned by the county or township authorities. They largely operate outside the limits of state control and produce goods for the local markets. They were the most dynamic sector of China's economy achieving phenomenal growth rates with an average of 45.5% a year between 1984 and 1988 according to International Monetany Fund (IMF) statistics.

The volume of recent literature on township industries does not do justice to its importance. China has reached the historical stage of development which Japan and the West went through in the past. This is the movement of farm workers to industrial occupations. In the West, this took the form of migration to the big cities. In China, strict control through residential permits checked such a population movement. So the surplus farm populations formed new townships.

With the aid of technology acquired through the technology markets or in other ways, township industries developed at an astonishing pace. These served China in two ways by absorbing large surplues of unemployed rural workers and by pushing economic growth to double-digit rates. That is why a growth rate of 3% or even 5%–6% aimed by the government will result in rapidly mounting unemployment in the countryside. Judith Banister, US Bureau of Census, quoted estimates of surplus rural labourers at between 60 million to 156 million in the 1980s.[5] China's Ministry of Labour estimates[6] that 11 million new jobs have to be created each year.[6] Lee Zinser places the number at 20 million.[7] Unless sufficient jobs are created, the political stability of the system will be threatened. This was the issue the 1989 Decision overlooked and what happened in 1990 provided a chastening experience.

Goh Keng Swee
2 September 1991

---

[5] Judith Banister, "China's Population changes and the Economy", in Joint Economic Committee, Congress of the US, *op. cit.*, Vol. 1, pp. 234–251. Several tables and charts cited in the text could not be found.

[6] *Xinhua News Agency,* 18 February 1991.

[7] Lee Zinser, "The Performance of China's Economy", in Joint Economic Committee, Congress of the US, *op. cit.*, pp. 135–159.

5

America Looks at China
Part IV — Correcting Systemic Weaknesses*

It is easy to come to misleading conclusions when examining a large and complex socio-economic system such as China, especially as the system is in a state of rapid change. Mistakes can stem from several sources.

The first is simply dogma to which, alas, intellectuals are sometimes prone. An example of this appears in Jan Prybyla's contribution.[1] He describes the Chinese economy not as a "mixed system" as did Robert Dernberger, but a mixed-up one. The economy is a confused economic order consisting of "disjointed bits and pieces ... lacking in internal logic and at odds with a reduced but still alive command bureaucracy."

In short, the economy amounts to a "non-system" which will lunge from crisis to crisis, alienating peasants, workers and intellectuals. Prybyla predicts a collapse within a few years. A reversion to central planning could postpone collapse by a decade but cannot prevent it. The

---

*Published by IEAP as *IEAP Discussion Paper No. 11* on 27 September 1991.
[1] Jan Prybyla, "A Systemic Analysis of Prospects for China's Economy", in Joint Economic Committee, Congress of the US, *China's Economic Dilemmas in the 1990s: The Problems of Reforms, Modernization, and Interdependence*, (Washington DC, US Govt Printing Office, 1991), Vol. 1, pp. 209–225.

author plainly believes that any major departure from the free enterprise system will bring early and unavoidable ruin.

The performance of China's economy in 1991 does not bear out Prybyla's forebodings. Exports in the first half of 1991 rose to US$29.25 billion, an increase of 17.5% resulting in a trade surplus of US$9 billion. In fact, China's predicament is her huge trade surplus with the US, which reached US$2.5 billion in the first four months. Not a bad performance for a non-system! The World Bank recently reported that China's per capita GNP doubled in ten years whereas mature industrial economies at a similar stage took more than 30 years to do so.[2]

Another source of error comes from what may be termed as the perspective of the observer. Some contributors see China in terms of opportunities for market penetration by American business and tend to regard obstacles to market penetration as systemic weaknesses. Such is the position taken by Martin Weil, US–China Business Council for US–China Joint Economic Committee 1990 Compendium[3] and William A. Fisher, Professor of Business Administration, University of North Carolina.[4] Fischer states that China should not depend on export-led growth because Western markets are less hospitable today than twenty years ago.

Low wages do not constitute a compelling advantage because industrial countries increasingly resort to automation. Instead, China's comparative advantage lies in her large domestic market and this should be used to attract foreign investors. In this way, China will better be able to absorb modern technology, practise modern management systems and establish a market economy. But Fischer ignored one difficulty — how profits from domestic sales in renminbi can be converted into hard currency for repatriation when this policy must result in chronic, large trade deficits.

---

[2] *World Bank Report*, "World Development Report, 1991: The Challenge of Development", pp. 12–13.

[3] Martin Weil, "The Business Climate in China: Half Empty or Half Full?", in Joint Economic, Congress of the US, *op.cit.*, Vol. 2, pp. 770–784.

[4] William A. Fisher, "China's Potential for Export-Led Growth", in Joint Economic Committee, Congress of the US, *op.cit.*, pp. 785–794.

A more fruitful approach was taken by Lee Zinser, Office of East Asian Analysis, CIA, and Barry Naughton, University of California at San Diego. They tried to find the causes of why the reform decade ended in the disasters of 1988–1989 inflation, corruption and intelligentsia unrest. Lee Zinser noted that currency in circulation increased by 47% in 1988.[5]

This huge spurt was the tip of the iceberg. During the reform decade, the decentralisation of authority and incentives to enterprise resulted in substantial loss of revenue to the central government. The ensuing budget deficits were financed partly by bond issues but increasingly by Central Bank credit and note issue. Inflation thus became unavoidable.

Barry Naughton points to a fatal institution weakness in China's banking system. Banks remain open to interference by powerful politicians. He noted, "Government and party officials are deeply involved in economic management at every level, and without checks on political power, these officials are subject to constant temptation to coerce banks to lend for their pet projects."[6]

Decentralisation of authority placed loan decisions in the hands of provincial and city officials. The result was a great surge of bank lending in provinces and localities. This dangerous situation was aggravated by the low reserve requirements placed by the Central Bank on commercial banks so that a given increase in bank deposits enables banks to expand loans by a large multiple of that increase. If they make bad loans, commercial banks in China do not go bankrupt as losses are made good by the state. So banks have no incentive to lend prudently and resist political pressure.

When in late 1988, the State Council introduced a national retrenchment programme, Barry Naughton notes that the impact of the credit squeeze on state enterprises took unexpected forms. Many stopped paying suppliers and piled up debts. They also stopped paying taxes and loan servicing obligations. Arrears on taxes and loan

---

[5] Lee Zinser, "The Performance of China's Economy", in Joint Economic Committee, Congress of the US, *op.cit.*, Vol. 1, pp. 102–118.
[6] Barry Naughton, "Inflation: Patterns, Causes and Cures", in Joint Economic Committee, Congress of the US, *op. cit.*, pp. 135–159.

obligations increased by 72% in 1989. No staff was retrenched nor their pay reduced. Bonuses were maintained where cash flow allowed. Since state enterprises cannot go bankrupt, the managements expect that eventually unpaid loans will be forgiven.

James B. Stepanek, Visiting Lecturer, Yale School of Organisation and Management, confirmed that the credit crunch did not affect state enterprises adversely.[7] What happened was that in 1990, subsidies to state enterprises were double the 1989 figure. Stepanek is a businessman with much experience in China and his account of how state enterprises function adds to our understanding of how intractable China's economic problems are.

State enterprises, when profitable, provide the central government with most of its revenue. The state ensures that the best engineers are assigned to them and they get preferred access to supplies of oil, coal, steel, foreign exchange, water and electricity. Though these are in short supply, they are much cheaper than that in the US, between a quarter to a twelfth of New England prices.

A state enterprise is more than a producing unit. Stepanek cites the example of Capital Iron and Steel Corporation in West Beijing. It has a work force of 135,000 of which only 15,000 are steel workers. The rest work in schools for employees' children, and in bakeries, theatres, or drive buses and grow vegetables and rice, etc. A power station in Liaoning has a work force of 3,000 of which 120 engineers and technicians run the station. A fibre glass factory in Badaling "fails to turn out quality panels for passenger trains, but the workers eat fresh fish because the plant director allows them a lot of time fishing at the Guanting Reservoir".

Singaporeans equate business with efficiency and may find it difficult to believe Stepanek's account. Though one cannot be sure of Stepanek's figures, foreign eye-witness' accounts provide corroborative evidence. The reality is widely recognised in China. A phrase has been coined to describe it — "Danwei (unit or employer) Socialism".

---

[7] James B. Stepanek, "China's Enduring State Factories: Why Ten Years of Reform Has Left China's Big State Factories Unchanged", in Joint Economic Committee, Congress of the US, *op. cit.*, Vol. 2, pp. 440–454.

Well-known terms such as "Iron-Rice Bowl" and "eating from the same big pot" were coined as pejorative characterisations of Danwei Socialism.

The World Bank regularly advises the Chinese government to get state enterprises to divest themselves of non-producing services, beginning with housing. The Chinese press urge danweis to lease retail shops and restaurants to private individuals. These practices are widely recognised as major obstacles to modernising China's econo-my. How is it that a decade of reform has made no dent here?

Stepanek believes the reason is mainly political. Too many people would lose their jobs if factories concentrated on production. Who would employ the bakers, teachers, cooks, nurses and others removed from the *danwei*'s payroll? Until a national social security system can take care of the unemployed, sick, hungry and uninsured, the state is reluctant to permit managers to fire workers. When the credit crunch of 1989 had taken its toll of less favoured enterprises, such as private firms, collectives and township enterprises, the first rescue package, amounting to US$1.7 billion was given to a preferred list of large state enterprises. "Is it any wonder" asked the writer, "that China's state enterprises don't change?"

We should not forget that the 1989 Decision of the Central Committee, a work of Party ideologues, singled out large state enterprises for privileged treatment on the ground that they formed the backbone of the national economy. How can the ideologues be so removed from reality? Is it only a matter of dogma? Clearly there are powerful underlying pressures that favour the maintenance of stability of institutions to the extent that obvious defects cannot be corrected.

Is it more than the fear of chaos (in Chinese *luan*), a pervasive sentiment among the population? The fear of chaos can be powerful only if chaos is, in fact, judged by intelligent people to be a real possibility. There is evidence that such a judgement is widely shared. For instance, it expresses itself in the idiom: 一抓就死, 一放就乱 (control results in stagnation, liberalisation in chaos).

This idiom is a good starting point for investigating the reason for Chinese fear of chaos. Even though the context here relates to the economy, unresolved economic problems can quickly deteriorate into political disorder. The Tiananmen Incident provides dramatic confirmation.

Chinese leaders and their advisers experience great difficulty in judging the impact of major economic reforms. This difficulty arises because important economic decisions are made on political grounds, for instance, the allocation of investment funds. Political decisions are inherently difficult, if not impossible, to predict, being essentially discretionary. In modern market economies where behaviour follows business calculations, the effect of policy is easier to predict. The inability to predict with confidence the outcome of major changes of economic policy makes the leadership extremely wary of making these changes, especially after Tiananmen. Even when these are seen as necessary because of the political costs few dare to change institutions such as *danwei* socialism practised by state enterprises.

We should carry the argument a stage further and ask why and how the Chinese system reached this condition. Of the contributors to the study, Kenneth Lieberthal offers the deepest insights.[8] Lieberthal traces China's systemic weaknesses to two sources. First, the centralization of power in a Leninist-type Party. Second, the historical legacy of the late Qing period.

The Leninist Party, characterised by a top-down command system, easily loses contact with reality as happened with the Great Leap Forward and the Cultural Revolution. Even in normal times, poor flows of information resulting from party control impede decision making at all levels of the administration. These arguments are well known and generally accepted.

The heritage of the late Qing compounds the difficulties produced by the Leninist-type authority structure. Lieberthal describes five ways in which this takes place. The late Qing did no serious work in setting up a legal system that could provide the huge country with a federal system. China is too large a country to be governed as a

---

[8] Kenneth Lieberthal, "The Dynamics of Internal Policies", in Joint Economic Committee, Congress of the US, *op. cit.*, Vol. 1, pp. 15–28.

unitary state once it progresses beyond an agricultural society. Under a federal system, it could decentralise authority to provinces in a stable way. Delegated authority is defined in precise legal terms and differences between centre and localities can be settled by an independent judiciary. In China, all major disputes between the centre and provinces have to be settled by negotiations, usually lengthy and acrimonious.

Second, the Qing never produced an effective system of central taxation. Taxes were farmed out to provinces and localities with central's share determined by negotiations. This remains substantially the position today. The results have been described in previous articles.

Third, the status of the military remained ambiguous under the late Qing which was faced with widespread disorders. Today, the military remains under the control of the Party and not the government, and the relation between civilian and military leaders remains unclear.

Fourth, the problem of personal power and lack of institutional constraints observed in China today has its origins in the late Qing when personal politics and factionalism undermined the institutional discipline of the traditional Chinese imperial civil service.

Fifth, foreign onslaughts during the late Qing contributed to a breakdown of China's core values relating to fundamental issues such as the basis of unity the government should seek. Lieberthal states that the political debates of 1988–1990 "included in a fairly prominent fashion virtually every basic perspective that was being hotly contested at the end of the Qing".

This last legacy of the late Qing will exert a more decisive influence on the future course of events than the other four. In an important sense, once a national consensus has emerged on core values, the others can be resolved as technical issues. The same conflict of opinion in political debates can be seen in debates on economic policies.

The divide is not between ideologues and reformers. Such a dichotomy oversimplifies. Among the reformers can be found scholars who are as well-versed in economic analysis as the liberal free marketeers in the West. There are also reform economists who approve of market guidance of enterprises only if the state has the power to "properly" control the market. These have not shaken off what Friedrich von Hayek calls the "fatal conceit of socialism" — the belief that persons in authority can have sufficient knowledge to make better judgements than the market.

This discord among the experts can have a major impact on the course of events. An ill-fated example occurred in January 1988 when the state arranged a national conference of economists to recommend what should be done to curb inflation, then running at 9%. While some of the reformists got the answers right — growth of money supply should be reined in — the ideologues opposed them. Ideologues argued that price increases indicated a shortage of goods and therefore more goods should be produced. Money supply should not be curbed as this was bound to reduce the output of goods. Faced with conflicting expert recommendations, the government temporised until inflation reached 29% in late summer, setting in train the events ending in the Tiananmen Incident.

The same sharp disagreement among the experts was responsible for the about-face of economic policies between November 1989 and December 1990 when the direction switched from pro-ideologue to pro-reformist. In the present state of uncertainty, decision-makers are likely to play it by ear, avoiding strong and decisive measures whose outcome they cannot foresee. For some time we are likely to see a policy of drift, at least in the centre. Provinces led by determined leaders may test their luck again to see how far they can go.

The American scholars are likely to be right in their judgement that, in the foreseeable future, the Chinese government will try to "muddle through". Given the robust potential for growth, this line of action may not lead to disaster but the full potential will not be achieved either. There is also the risk that unattended small troubles will pile up into big ones.

While the leaders are in a temporising mood, one should note that they have no intention of following the Soviet Union's renunciation of Marxism. They understand that Marxist ideology provides the basis of legitimacy of Communist rule. Once ideology is abandoned, the whole edifice of state power begins to crumble. So while Chinese leaders search for a way out of their difficulties, they believe that the search has greater chances of success if the structure of state authority remains intact.

China will avoid the upheavals which recently occurred in the Soviet Union. But their approach leaves them with a trade-off between ideology and economic progress. China's dilemma is that ideology advances stability but impedes progress. In Singapore, political stability and economic progress go together but this is not always the case in China as numerous examples in this series demonstrate. In the years ahead, the skill with which the leaders manage this trade-off should be watched with interest. Managing the trade-off will be less troublesome when the Long March generation leave the scene.

Goh Keng Swee
2 September 1991

6

Li Peng on China's State Enterprises*

Editors' Note

SOEs (state-owned enterprises) in all socialist economies are notorious for their inefficiency and wastefulness mainly because they operate under the so-called "soft budget constraint". China at that time had more than 40,000 SOEs, 10,000 of which were large and medium-sized enterprises. This state sector constituted the mainstay of the economy. In the transition from central planning to a market system, the single most important issue is, therefore, the reform of the SOEs.

Economists can easily and cogently argue their case for SOE reform based on the mainstream economic theory. But the ways and means of doing this can be immensely difficult. Different governments would follow different policy prescriptions, much depending on their ideological inclination and institutional requirement. Suffice it to say that this is the topic with which Goh Keng Swee was very much at home, both as a good economist himself and as a policy maker who had been personally involved in developing and managing Singapore's own SOEs, known as GLCs (government-linked companies).

In March 1991, Chinese Premier Li Peng, a well-known conservative, put forth his views and policies for reforming China's SOEs. Goh closely tracked Li's policy announcements and discussed them in the broader context of China's existing economic reform progress and potential challenges.

Li's approach to SOE reform was cautious, too cautious in fact, mainly calling for modernising management and upgrading production technology. Goh was quick to foresee that such partial reform could offer only a

---

*Published by IEAP as *IEAP Discussion Paper No. 14* on 21 December 1991.

short-term remedy. A fundamental solution to tackle the SOE reform would need some radical policies, including breaking the "Iron Rice Bowl" (permanent employment) of the workers. Goh had concluded that the implementation of such thorough-going reform policies would have to wait for the "future generation of enlightened leaders".

Indeed, China's SOE reform has been a long-drawn-out process. After Li Peng, Premier Zhu Rongji picked up the challenge, went much further and achieved a breakthrough. But China today is still facing some challenges from its existing SOEs — now just a little over 100 in number.

Prologue

Statement of the Problem

"Excessive consumption (of energy and materials) in production, inferior quality, enormous waste in construction, slow capital turnover, low labour productivity and serious enterprise losses are to be found everywhere... since we shall continue to be plagued by a huge population, heavy construction tasks, shortage of funds, outdated basic industries and infrastructure, and relatively inadequate resources in terms of average per-capita amount, we shall get nowhere relying on poor management which wastes resources."

Solution A

"Upgrading technology is the chief means we have for improving economic performance... during the coming decade, we must update existing enterprises with advanced technology, equipment and production techniques, and tackle key problems in scientific research and prodution, focusing on production technology and modern equipment."

Solutin B

"At present, financial, material and human resources are recklessly wasted in production, construction and trade, and the development potential in these areas is far from being tapped. Therefore, we must make tighter management the key link in improving economic performance..."

1. Introduction

The collapse of the Sovient Union and Eastern Europe can be traced to one basic cause — the appalling inefficiency of socialist state enterprises. It is perhaps no coincidence that this year the Chinese government is making a concentrated effort to improve her state industries. This paper discusses the measures proposed by Premier Li Peng to achieve this. Part I describes these proposals — eleven major ones and nine ancillaries.

Part II assesses the chances of successful outcome. Insofar as the present troubles derived from backward technology, the installation of new machinery, including imports, will improve production. This will especially apply to industries identified by the government as creating bottlenecks in production — energy, raw materials and semi-finished goods, transportation and telecommunications. However, so long as the prices of these are kept artificially low, these industries will continue to depend on state financial and other assistance. If their prices are raised to world levels, it will generate a huge cost-push inflation. China's fear of inflation remains the main obstacle to price reforms.

In applying technology to promote long-term industrial transformation, China will not be able to reproduce Japan's post-war success story. She lacks the three institutions which enabled Japan to identify sunrise technologies and transform laboratory breakthroughs into mass-produced high-quality products. These are her worldwide reporting systems based on her trading companies, the symbiotic grouping of banking, manufacturing and trading eneterprises into keiretsu combines, and third, the unique Japanese system of information dissemination.

The second route to improving state enterprises, that is, through improved management, is strewn with insuperable difficulties, much of which result from the ideological baggage their leaders carry, such as egalitarian income distribution, welfare services provided by state enterprises, special status of workers, permanent employment, etc. Rapid changes in these areas run a big risk of social discontent. It is therefore unlikely that the Chinese will resort to the precipitate action we now see in the former Soviet Union.

If China wishes to reach world economic standards, the reforms to the system must be brought to completion by a future generation of leaders. Part III briefly notes the essential elements. Price reforms must be pushed ahead; the impact of the resultant cost-push inflation can be eased by wage indexation. The welfare functions now performed by state enterprises — housing, education, health services, pensions — should be transferred to local authorities. A free labour market should replace the iron-rice bowl. A free capital market based on an independent central bank and commercial banks responsible for profits and losses should replace the present system of fund allocation based mainly on political grounds.

Implementation of these reforms goes beyond the capabilities of the present political and government institutions. Reforms to these will be needed, but they run counter to cherished dogma. Political reforms include a Federal Constitution defining limits of authority, a modern judicial system to settle disputes between center and province, and a professional civil service that can resist political pressure. A future generation of enlightened leaders will see the necessity of these reforms and undertake them.

2. Proposed Remedies

This year, Premier Li Peng spoke about improving the performance of large- and medium-sized state enterprises (LMSEs) on no less than five occasions.[1] The last occasion was on 23 September 1991 when he

---

[1] The occasions were: (i) 12 February 1991, address to the Closing Session of the National Enterprises Work Conference; (ii) 25 March 1991, report to the National People's Congress; (iii) 23 May 1991, Address to the National Work Conference on Economic Structural Reform in a speech "Further Deepen Reform, Invigorate Large and Medium-sized Enterprises"; (iv) 1 August 1991, Address to the 11th Plenary Session of the State Council on the General Economic Situation; (v) 23 September 1991, address to the Central Committee of the Communist Party of China (Full text published in *Renmin Ribao*, 11 October 1991). These speeches are cited in the following pages by the number used in this footnote, e.g. Li Peng: (iv) refers to the 1 August 1991 speech to the State Council.

addressed the Cental Work Conference and the full text was published in *Renmin Ribao* (*People's Daily*) on 11 October 1991. Subsequently, a flurry of articles and speeches by important leaders followed — no less than five were published in the 28 October 1991 issue of *Renmin Ribao*.

The reason for this concern is not difficult to see. The ideologues who dominated policy making in 1989 had set out in November of that year in the clearest terms possible the type of economic system they preferred.[2] LMSEs are the backbone of a socialist economy and they must be strengthened by preferential treatment in the allocation of funds and physical resources. They must also be protected from competition from township enterprises.

The measures intended to strengthen LMSEs produced the opposite results. Preferential treatment instead of improving LMSEs performance resulted in greater losses, and larger stockpiles of unsold goods, etc. Increased state subsidies had to be paid to them and this created serious budgetary difficulties in 1990. So the Central Committee reversed course in their "Proposal" adopted on 30 December 1990.[3] The rapid deterioration of the economy in 1990 was too widespread and too evident for the leadership to take any other course.

Premier Li Peng's preoccupation with LMSEs shows that he intends to strengthen the socialist economic system — as the ideologues conceive it and when successful, return to the policies advanced in the Decision of 1989 which collapsed because of far-reaching weaknesses of LMSEs. What he says and the outcome of policies he advances to redress these weaknesses will therefore have an important bearing on the course of events in the next few years.

Premier Li's first systematic exposition of methods of invigorating LMSEs was given on 23 May 1991 when he addressed the National

---

[2] See "Decision of the Central Committee of the Communist Party on Economic Policy, 9 November 1989", *IEAP Internal Discussion Paper No. 1*, 21 May 1991.

[3] Eu Chooi Yip, "Chinese Reformers Regain the High Ground", *IEAP Discussion Paper No. 5*, 7 June 1991.

Work Conference on Economic Structural Reform.[4] He classified his recommendations under 11 headings, briefly explained as follows:

(i) Technology upgrading. This means the purchase of new, including imported, machinery and equipment. Such purchases could be financed by concessionary loans and special allocation of foreign exchange to selected LMSEs.

(ii) Selected LMSEs to be allowed higher rates of depreciation. Enterprises in China are allowed to retain their depreciation funds and enjoy a measure of autonomy in the use of these funds for capital investment and technology upgrading.

(iii) Reduce the rate of interest on bank deposits and loans. The recent sharp increases in interest rates to take into account high rates of inflation in 1988–89, found little favour among ideologues. With the decline in inflation, interest rates have gone down.

(iv) Selected LMSEs should be allowed to handle their own foreign trade. At present both imports and exports of goods and materials are handled by specialised trading companies, most of which are controlled by the Ministry of Foreign Economic Relations and Trade (MOFERT). LMSEs do not deal directly with suppliers of machinery or equipment nor with foreign purchasers for their exports. This change will enable LMSEs to retain a larger percentage of hard currency earnings from their exports. Direct dealings with foreign suppliers and importers, a common practice in free enterprise contracts, can be advantageous to LMSE managements in widening their horizons.

(v) Mandatory plans for selected LMSEs to be reduced. In effect this means that LMSEs will be able to sell a higher portion of their output in the open market at a higher price. Liberalisation of the economy has obvious merits irrespective of their impact on LMSE efficiency.

(vi) Increase working capital for some LMSEs. The effects of the 1988–1990 credit crunch has not worn out, so selected LMSEs will be offered larger bank credit to ease financial constraints.

---

[4] Li Peng: (iii).

(vii) Increase funds for developing new products. One of the prominent features of LMSEs is their disinclination to introduce new or improved products, unlike enterprises in capitalist countries. This recommendation therefore aims at correcting this inequality in performance.

(viii) Burdens placed on LMSEs to be reduced. In other speeches, Premier Li explained that this refers to fees, charges and taxes which local authorities arbitrarily levy on enterprises operating in their area of jurisdiction.[5]

(ix) Break the debt chain. A separate IEAP paper explains the predicament most enterprises in China find themselves in resulting from the austerity measures of 1988–1989.[6]

(x) Establish LMSE groups. Premier Li elaborated on this proposal to distinguish it from mergers and takeovers. The object of the grouping of LMSEs is to raise efficiency through:

(a) Unified production, supply and marketing operations.
(b) Unified manpower and financial management.
(c) Improved technology transfer.

The recent "shareholding" system under which enterprises can issue shares in the stock markets in Shanghai and Shenzhen is seen as a mechanism to promote such grouping. However, it is not clear whether he had in mind what we call "vertical integration", i.e. combining firms engaged in various stages of production, e.g. vehicle production combining with parts manufacturers. It could also be that he was thinking of "horizontal integration", combination of firms producing similar goods so that they form a sort of cartel. Another possibility is that this idea was inspired by the Japanese institutions of "keiretsu" grouping of manufacturers, suppliers, trading houses and banks.

---

[5] Li Peng: (i) and (ii).

[6] Zou Ziying, "Debt Chains in China", *IEAP Background Brief No. 20*, 5 December 1991. In three months, from July to September 1991, no less than five conferences were held on this subject. These conferences were of sufficient importance to merit lengthy reporting in BBC Summary of World Broadcasts and the US Foreign Broadcasting Information Service.

(xi) The last item refers to the "Double Guarantee" system under which the state guarantees to supply stated amounts of raw materials to 234 LMSEs which guarantee the supply of agreed amounts of finished products.

In other speeches, Premier Li described other measures (see Annex 1 for a table setting out the occasions on which the most important proposals of Premier Li were made). These included:

(i) To improve the contract responsibility system under which LMSEs operate. Under this system (experimentally introduced in 1979 and adopted nation-wide in 1987), certain performance targets are negotiated between LMSEs and state supervisory bureaus for a period of three or more years. Targets set vary according to circumstances and include such matters as product mix, quantities of output, proportion for delivery to state and for open market, supplies of raw materials from state and open sources, level of profits and amounts of taxes, new capital expenditure, etc. One innovation proposed by Premier Li is to calculate profits before the deduction of loan repayments. Hitherto, China used the unique method of allowing debt capital repayments to be charged against pre-tax profits with consequent loss to the state revenue.

(ii) Separate ownership from management. This is a hardy perennial intended to protect management from outside interference. The constant repetition of the theme suggests that the objective remains elusive.

(iii) Define functions of Party Committee and LMSEs management so that they work together for the common good. Another hardy perennial and equally suggestive of the lack of success.

(iv) Reduce overstocking. This merely means that LMSEs should stop producing unwanted goods.[7]

---

[7] These goods include bicycles, mechanical watches, refrigerators, washing machines, electric fans and electric irons. To a lesser extent, shoes, liquor, furniture, plastic products, processed foods and paper. Inventories at end June 1991 amounted to 44 billion *yuan*, nearly double the normal level, according to Yu Zhen, Vice-Minister, Ministry of Light Industry, *China ®Daily*, 16 September 1991.

   (v) Increase tax payments and profits.
  (vi) Reduce the number of loss-making LMSEs.
 (vii) Reduce energy and material inputs in production.
(viii) Stop excessive wage increases.
  (ix) Increase market guidance.

All these recommendations are commendable. However, the difficulty lies in how to carry them out. On 1 August 1991, Premier Li made a progress report to the State Council on the 11-point Plan issued in May. Projects for technology upgrading had already been selected and they "must be carried out to the letter". Three of the eleven proposals were in force, another six were in process of implementation and two had yet to start. He expressed confidence that the 11-point Plan "can produce the desired results".[8]

The following month when he reported to the CPC Central Committee on 23 September 1991, he sounded less optimistic. He said, "The trend of low economic efficiency has not yet been reversed. Profits of enterprises have been on the decline, while stockpiles of production have continued to rise and debt defaults still throttle industry."[9] He also pointed out that state budget deficits continued to rise.

His general conclusion was that the general economic structure remained unbalanced with non-state enterprises "taking relatively too large a part of the nation's energy and raw materials at the expense of the state sector because of poor efficiency of some LMSEs.[10]

Four months' experience with the 11-point Plan is too short to pass judgement. As early as February 1991, Premier Li pointed out: "Raising enterprise efficiency is a formidable and protracted task which cannot be accomplished in one or two years."[11] From this, we can infer that the effort to improve LMSE efficiency will remain state policy as long as Premier Li retains his position. It would therefore be useful to assess the Plan's prospects.

---

[8] Li Peng: (iv).
[9] Li Peng: (v).
[10] Li Peng: (v).
[11] Li Peng: (i).

3. Will They Work?

One can evaluate the 11-point Plan from two perspectives. The first accepts what is possible and practical in the existing political and economic framework governing the operations of China's economy. The second takes a broader view by comparing the Plan with what can happen in a free enterprise economy. Of course, the second perspective may be faulted as unrealistic and unfair as it judges the operations of one system by criteria appropriate to a different one. Nevertheless, the exercise is not without value for two reasons. First, it throws light on what further reforms are needed before LMSEs can hope to operate at the same level of efficiency achieved by capitalist enterprises. Second, the industrial output of township enterprises — the aggregate value of which was recently reported to have exceeded that of LMSEs — was produced under competitive conditions not greatly dissimilar from the free enterprise system. In other words, a comparison between efficiency of capitalist and socialist enterprises has relevance in China. People can see for themselves the relative merits of these two systems of production found in China.

Starting with the first approach, we must accept that Premier Li's proposals are based on the best information available on LMSEs and the specific measures have taken into account what is acceptable given the mind set of implementing bureaucracies and the customary-operating procedures of LMSEs' management. This explains the inclusion of stale items such as safeguards against outside interference and relations between party and enterprise management.

The sheer size of China's problems reaches intimidating proportions. Whereas Singapore has a few scores of government linked companies (GLCs), the Chinese have more than 40,000 of which more than 10,000 consist of LMSEs, spread over 30 provinces. They produce a wide range of goods, from strategic nuclear missiles to cotton yarn.

As the prologue indicates, Premier Li bases his strategy on improvements in two critical areas: (a) better production system through using advanced technology and (b) improvements to the present inefficient management system.

Economists are inclined to dismiss the introduction of advanced technology as an engineer's solution to an economic problem. No doubt there have been instances where advanced technology had been mistakenly applied, for instance, in many show-piece development projects in capital-hungry Third World countries. But for long-term development of an industrial system, technology upgrading plays a decisive role provided resources are allocated to the right industries.

Therefore, the critical issue here is whether governments can be entrusted to make the right decisions on resource allocation or whether such decisions should best be left to the market. Free market economists hold decisive views on the subject and produce plenty of evidence from Third World experience of official ineptitude and folly. Yet the example of Japan in the first two or three post-war decades showed that correct decisions on resource allocation in technology upgrading can be made by government. Japan at the time had to import advanced technology by buying industrial know-how from the West. This was done by licensing agreements between Japanese firms and American and European enterprises.[12] Since Japan then suffered from chronic shortages of foreign exchange, Japanese firms had to get official approval for licensing agreements. The Japanese government had a broad idea of what industrial priorities would produce the best long-term results. Japan has demonstrated that, under certain circumstances, the government can make wise choices on resource allocation. The question therefore arises: "Can the Chinese government do the same?"

In principle, there is no reason why they cannot. Making correct the decisions on priorities depends on the ability in performing two functions. The first is getting information on requirements of enterprises in relation to available resources. In China's case, resources refer mainly to hard currency and domestic technical skills, both of which are scarce in relation to needs. The second is making sound judgement on the future course of technology developments. On the first function, the system in China is probably not inferior to post-war Japan.

---

[12] Matsunaga Yoshio, *Successful Licensing To and From Japan*, Nihon Brain Corporation, 1974.

The Chinese government has a clear idea of which industries stand in greatest need of technology upgrading.[13] We should also note that in China, unlike Japan and the West, the government cannot depend on market forces to make these decisions as the market gives confusing signals. This will continue to be so until price reforms are completed. The needs of the moment, however, are not in doubt. In three areas, supply bottlenecks caused chronic problems in downstream industries. These areas are:

 (i) Energy — output of coal, oil and electricity.
 (ii) Semi-finished goods such as iron and steel, and non-ferrous metals.
(iii) Transportation services by road, rail, water and air.

It should be noted that the bulk of production in these three areas is carried on by LMSEs. These are plagued by inefficient management, as is well known, but in addition because they produce what economic planners consider "strategic goods and services", policy makers insist that their prices must be kept low. As a result, they experience great difficulty in accumulating funds for expansion of output and have to rely on the state budget. Policy makers are reluctant to sanction realistic price increases because of two fears. The immediate fear is that the users, i.e. downstream industries, will experience financial difficulty unless they too can pass on price increases to their customers. The long-term fear is that when eventually these price increases are absorbed down the production stream, this will ignite a large cost-push inflation. But without market prices which reflect scarcities in relation to costs, these "strategic industries" will continue to depend on the state support for investment funds. They cannot mount self-generating expansion through accumulated retained profits and long-term loans raised in the money markets.

As regards the second point, it is unlikely that the Chinese government can reach the same level of competence achieved by the Japanese in making judgements on the future development of

---

[13] Goh Keng Swee, "America Looks at China Part III — Absorbing Modern Technology", *IEAP Disscussion Paper No. 11*, 20 September 1991.

technology. Japanese excellence in this field is probably unequalled among industrial nations. It rests on the solid foundation of three Japanese institutions. The first consists of the large network of trading companies such as Mitsubishi, Mitsui, Sumitomo, Marubeni, etc. These companies station experienced staff in all countries with whom trading relations have been established. These staff members make it part of their mission to study and report not only on trade opportunities but also on significant technology progress made in their host countries. The second institution is the grouping of industrial enterprises around trading companies and banks — the keiretsu. This eases the despatch of experts for on-the-spot examination of interesting technology breakthroughs. Follow-up action can be quickly initiated when called for. The third institution is the Japanese system of efficient dissemination of information flows throughout the economy.

China lacks all these. Her foreign trade representation abroad still remains at a rudimentary level. No discernable equivalent of the keiretsu has emerged and the Chinese practice is to hoard useful information rather than disseminate it. It is an inescapable consequence of this that China's policy on technology upgrading will be confined to addressing current difficulties in troubled areas. The forward-looking Japanese strategy of broad advance is beyond their present competence. Where the Chinese focus attention on high technology areas such as mirco-electronics and genetic engineering, they will achieve success because of the high quality of their scientists. But such successes will remain isolated and not result in the kind of spectacular commercialisation of research discoveries achieved by the Japanese.

The second objective — improving LMSE management — will not be attained. Many of the measures proposed had been tried before with disappointing results. They do not address the basic causes of inefficient management. While the reforms of 1984 to 1987 — introducing the contract responsibility system, separating party from management responsibilities and reducing the scope of mandatory planning — had given a great boost to production, the effects wore out and some of the bad habits of the past reasserted themselves. These bad habits may be considered under three headings.

First, the iron-rice bowl. This results from the absence of a labour market, the assignment of workers to enterprises by the local Labour Bureau and the virtual impossibility of dismissing workers on grounds of inefficiency. LMSEs in addition provide a wide range of welfare services ranging from housing to schools, hospitals, pensions, shops, restaurants, etc, depending on their affluence. A large state enterprise becomes a small welfare state. There has been no serious attempt to dismantle the welfare state. One reason could be the multitude of redundant employees.

Second, the pervading egalitarian ethos prevents LMSEs from observing State Council's injunction to link pay and bonuses to workers' output. Thus, profits distributed as bonuses are usually shared equally. Even when losses are made, bonuses could still be distributed on the grounds that losses were caused by outside events beyond the control of the enterprise and are that workers in the enterprise work as hard as others and are therefore equally deserving of bonus payments. Managers and party branches cannot discipline workers because they have officially been designated "masters of the enterprise". Since loss-making LMSEs can depend on state subsidies, incentives to management and workers to improve performance remain weak. The result of all these arrangements is that increases in personal income outstrips increases in productivity, as Premier Li had repeatedly complained.[14]

The third impediment to efficient management is found in the partial state of price reform. While the Premier urged LMSEs to

---

[14] Li Peng: (iii). "The third difficulty is caused by last year's wage rise for staff members and workers of enterprises." The other two were the cancellation of construction projects and over capacity in the machine-building industry.

Li Peng: (iv). "We must see to it that... the increases in real average income does not outstrip that of labour productivity."

Li Peng: (v). "The rate of increase in the incomes of workers and staff members is higher than the production growth rate and distribution favours the individual. Many enterprises guarantee two things — tax payments as well as bonus and other welfare benefits — at the expense of technological transformation and development of new products."

increase their dependence on market guidance, the market can only give confused signals. With the two-tier price system and state guidance of prices of goods produced for the market, dependence on market guidance encourages corruption as well as efficiency. The real difficulty over prices has been mentioned before. LMSEs are concentrated in the production of "strategic goods", the prices of which are kept low.

The purpose of market guidance goes beyond telling LMSEs what to produce. Where all prices — including factor prices such as wages and salaries and interest on capital — are determined in a competitive market, market guidance identifies efficient producers from inefficient ones. The efficient prosper, expand, pay better wages and dividends and create more jobs. The inefficient close down. This does not happen among LMSEs. However, there are signs of increasing impatience over the three bad habits among the top leadership and the resort to bankruptcy laws is being recommended.

The principal deterrent to launching thorough-going economic reforms is the fear of social disruption that they will cause. The Chinese leaders are probably wise in carrying out reforms in stages. Despite the many flaws revealed in the process, marked progress in GNP growth had been achieved and standards of living have increased substantially.[15] It is unlikely that the present leaders in office will risk throwing away these achievements by making a dash for reforms in the way the Russians are doing.

4. Future Tasks

The completion of reforms will, therefore, be a task left to future generations of leaders. This is a task of immense size and complexity

---

[15] John Wong, "What is China's Per Capita GNP?", *IEAP Background Brief No. 18*, 18 October 1991. Western scholars applying the technique of Purchasing Power Parity estimated that China's per capital GNP was US$2,472 in 1988.

and we briefly indicate the main ingredients. At the core of the reforms are four necessary (though not sufficient) conditions:

(i) Price reforms must be completed and the hazards of a large cost-push inflation accepted as unavoidable. If properly managed by raising pay in keeping with inflation through a system of wage-indexing, this need not lead to social discontent.

(ii) LMSEs welfare states should be dismantled. These services could be taken over by local, provincial and central authorities. To the extent that these services are necessary, the change will involve a transfer of personnel from LMSEs to various authorities and the transfer of funds from LMSEs to takeover authorities equivalent to the expenditure they save in this exercise.

(iii) The iron-rice bowl to be broken by the establishment of a free labour market. Social discontent cannot be avoided but can be minimised to the extent the welfare functions described earlier have been transferred to authorities.

(iv) A free capital market to be set up, preceded by a reform of the banking system by the establishment of an independent central bank and with commercial banks run for profits.

It is unnecessary to argue these propositions in detail. All we need to note is that they cannot be successfully carried out in China without certain major changes to government institutions. To mention a few, first, there must be a professional civil service at central and provincial levels. Next, the present amorphous unitary constitution has to be replaced by a Federal Constitution clearly defining the authority and responsibilities of centre and province. Third, a modern judicial system should be set up which can do away with the long drawn out process of bargaining to settle disputes between center and province as well as province and lower authorities. The present relationship between the capital and the provinces does not differ in essentials from the imperial regimes set up since the Han dynasty. The imperial system served China well enough when there was a professional elite civil service administering a rural economy. A modern industrial system cannot operate under such a system, especially when there is no modern civil service and judiciary. These institutions conflict with many cherished tenets of socialism and they will take much time and effort to set up.

Annex 1

Proposals	When made				
1 Upgrade Technology	A		C	D	E
2 Raise Depreciation Rates	A		C		E
3 Reduce Rate of Interest	A		C		E
4 Some Enterprises to do Foreign Trade			C		E
5 Reduce Proportion for Sale at Controlled Prices			C		E
6 Increase Working Capital	A		C		E
7 Increase Funds to Develop New Products	A		C		E
8 Reduce Burdens of Illegal Local Charges	A	B	C		E
9 Break Debt Chain	A		C	D	E
10 Set up Enterprise Groups	A	B	C		E
11 Double Guarantees			C		E
12 Improve Contract Responsibility System	A	B			E
13 Separate Management from Ownership		B			
14 Define Party Committee and Management Functions	A	B			E
15 Reduce Overstocking	A			D	
16 Increase Tax Payments and Profits	A				
17 Reduce Number of Loss-making Enterprises	A				

(*Continued*)

(Continued)

Proposals	When made		
18 Reduce Energy and Material Inputs A			
19 Preferential Income Tax			E
20 Reform Wage System (Stop Excessive Wage Increases)	C	D	E
21 Increase market guidance			E

Note:

A: Li Peng: (i) 12 February 1991.

B: Li Peng: (ii) 25 March 1991.

C: Li Peng: (iii) 23 May 1991.

D: Li Peng: (iv) 1 August 1991.

E: Li Peng: (v) 23 September 1991.

7

Into the 21st Century*

Editors' Note

Goh Keng Swee was a learned man. His wide knowledge of world history is clearly manifested in this short speech at the conference of history teachers in 1994. After a brief discussion of modern history starting from the Industrial Revolution and a broad sweep of economic development in Southeast Asia, Goh turned to Russia and China. According to him, the main influence on the course of events in the 21st century would depend much on how Russia and China put their houses in order.

Gorbachev introduced glasnost and political reform, and this unleashed political and social forces that led to the final collapse of the Soviet Union in 1991. Economic reform in Russia was also not conspicuously successful because of the "Big Bang" approach it adopted. In contrast, China experienced no radical regime change and its economic reform was proceeding on a gradual basis through learning by doing. As a result, China's economic reform and economic development were much more successful. But China was also facing many economic problems due to its incomplete transition to a market economy. Beyond market reform, both Russia and China would still have to come to grip with their political reform. Their failure, in the words of Goh, "could be calamitous for the world".

---

*Speech delivered at the History Teachers' Conference in Singapore on 7 March 1994.

> The country ... which was large enough to support the original inhabitants, will now be too small. If we are to have enough pasture and plough land, we shall have to cut off a slice of our neighbour's territory; and if they too are not content with necessities, but give themselves to getting unlimited wealth, they will want a slice of our own.
>
> > That is inevitable, Socrates,
> > So the next thing will be, Glaucon, that we shall be at war.
>
> — *The Republic of Plato* (EM. Comford translation)

The starting point of what the 21st century will hold could be to describe the special features of this century, point out the most significant events and try to discover the underlying forces which brought about these events. To be sure, the causes are diverse and complex, but a certain logical and coherent order does emerge.

While different people will judge this period in different terms, I believe that the most appropriate way to sum-up this century is that it is an "Age of Violence". In the two world wars fought, more combatants were engaged than fighting in all wars in preceding centuries. Also more civilians have died than civilian deaths in all previous wars. Carpet bombing of cities, organized massacres of civilians by occupying troops were regular occurrences. In February 1942, Singapore suffered its share of military atrocities when Japanese troops massacred some 30,000 civilians.

The war finally ended in August 1945, when Hiroshima and Nagasaki were devastated by nuclear bombs which killed nearly a quarter million civilians. Somehow this seemed a fitting symbolic end to the greatest of wars fought in the "Age of Violence".

Confronted with these disturbing facts many questions will occur to a thinking person. Has 20th century society become more barbarous than people in ancient times, such as Genghis Khan or Attila? Could the last wars have been avoided? There are deeper issues — what are the causes of wars in the 20th century, particularly the two world wars? Most importantly, are the underlying forces that caused these wars still present and will they persist into the 21st century?

Let us answer the easy questions first. No, we have not on the whole become more barbarous than Genghis Khan or Attila. In their defence, historians have claimed that when civilians were killed, it was done out of military necessity — to terrify the region into submission without fighting. But Hitler, when he killed millions of civilians in the Holocaust, could not invoke the principle of military necessity. So the answer to this question must be a qualified one.

Could the war be avoided? Given the circumstances in 1939, the answer must be "probably not". This war was a continuation of the First World War of 1914–18. Some military historians claim that the earlier conflict was not a world war but a European civil war and the causes can best be understood if we take this position. We must briefly study why Europeans fight each other so frequently.

European societies traditionally were organised into separate states under a system of hereditary monarchy. Wars between these states were regular occurrences, but until the late 18th century, wars were fought by relatively small numbers of professional soldiers, usually for limited objectives, unless ideological issues were raised and wars of religion were unleashed.

Before the 18th century, we can say that many of the conflicts between European states could be traced to the desire to expand territory, although other factors did play a part, such as historical rivalry, desire for vengeance, religious quarrels, etc. Until the Industrial Revolution began in England in the late 18th century, wealth was created by ownership and cultivation of land. The kings, dukes, earls and barons were wealthy and powerful by virtue of ownership of land — hence their designation as "the landed aristocracy".

There is a simple economic reason for this. With unchanging technology, more output and, hence greater wealth required the cultivation of more land by more farm labourers.

As the Industrial Revolution unfolded an unending series of inventions, some intellectuals reacted with disapproval over social conditions in emerging industrial cities. Others saw it for what it was — a totally new means of creating wealth. Foremost among these thinkers were Adam Smith and Karl Marx. Their theories would have profound consequences in succeeding decades and centuries.

Adam Smith believed that production to meet the needs of a free competitive market unfettered by government intervention was the correct way to accumulate wealth. Karl Marx lived in a time when the factory towns displayed a sharp contrast between the wealthy few and the impoverished many and came to the opposite conclusion. He laid the philosophical basis for the overthrow of the capitalist system by the working class through a revolutionary seizure of power.

Instead of going to war to conquer lands, the Industrial Revolution enabled European states to concentrate on creating wealth through the application of science and technology to production instead of trying to take slices of each other's territory. Instead, they reached out to the world beyond and seized vast tracts of land in Asia and Africa.

Even as European states became richer through the efforts of their entrepreneurs and bankers, national rivalries remained, aggravated by two elements. First, some countries such as Germany grew faster than the others. Next, weapons increased in lethal power and countries devoted increasing expenditure on them. These developments produced both jealousy and fear. One outcome of this situation was the formation of alliances, a practice in which European diplomats had centuries of experience.

When the war engulfed the major European powers, it was a total war. Men were conscripted, women assigned to work in factories to produce ammunition, the whole society of every combatant country mobilised for the war effort. Nothing like this had happened before.

An early casualty of the war was Russia, then an absolute monarchy under an amiable mediocrity, Czar Nicholas II. He was deposed in January 1917 by Alexander Kerensky, whose provisional government in turn fell to Lenin's Bolshevik *coup* in November 1917. Lenin enjoyed the support of the war-weary armed forces because he promised to end the war while Kerensky pledged to continue the fight. Lenin immediately sued for peace, which the German granted under the Treaty of Brest Litovsk on 3 March 1918. Thus the first Marxist state was established.

Some accounts of Lenin's sudden appearance in Russia in April 1917 claim that he was smuggled in by the German Secret Service to knock Russia out of the war.

When the war ended in November 1918, the Europeans — noted for their belligerency in historical records as early as Thucydides' *Peloponnesian Wars* and Julius Caesar's *De Bello Gallico* — had enough of fighting. But their newly found mood of pacifism was not to last long. Wars produce winners and losers. The latter usually thirst for revenge. This was what happened when the Weimar Republic set up after the war by the victors was replaced by Adolf Hitler's Nazi regime in 1933. The Treaty of Versailles had kept the Germans not only virtually demilitarised but made them poor through punitive reparations. Dealing with so formidable a people in this way was not the ideal way to maintain peace, when the victors lacked the will to enforce the terms of the Treaty.

The Second World War was a continuation of the first, only on a grander scale involving much of Asia — Japan, China, Vietnam, Indonesia, Malaysia, Singapore, Burma, Sri Lanka and India. In all these conflicts, the USA did not acquire the world view of European countries brought about by centuries of historical rivalry. In fact, the early migrants left Britain because they disliked British institutions and political practices. Except for a brief period during which the USA took large chunks of territory from Mexico in what is now Texas and California, as well as the Philippines from Spain, they did not join in the European scramble to acquire overseas empires.

For the most part, Americans in the 19th century were absorbed with domestic affairs including a bloody civil war over the abolition of slavery. Theirs was an immensely large continent to settle people in; there were vast natural resources in minerals and energy to develop. They concentrated on encouraging immigration from Europe to provide workers for the great undertakings economic development required. Early in the process, Americans understood that improvements in education, especially at university level, yielded rich rewards.

In all these great enterprises — the setting up of industries and railway networks, exploration of oil and minerals, and even the establishment of universities before this century, the Americans believed that the responsibility should rest with private individuals, not the government. Adam Smith had become their patron saint.

The free enterprise system operating in the huge market of the USA allowed the industrial system to take full advantage of economies of large-scale production. Competition between giant corporations encouraged the investment of large sums in Research and Development as a means of beating competitors. In World War II, when the unique strength of the American system was applied to producing the weapons of war, a staggering flow of aircraft, guns, tanks, landing craft, aircraft carriers and finally the atomic bomb, emerged from American facilities and sealed the fate of the enemy.

The end of World War II did not bring world peace. The reason is that it did not bring an end to rivalry between states. The vanquished were treated with a magnanimity absent in the previous war. So Germany and Japan were able to emerge from the devastation inflicted on them by the war and in a few decades produced their economic miracles. This time, state rivalry arose among the victors — America and her democratic allies on the one side and the Soviet Union and her Communist allies on the other. Another Marxist state emerged four years after the end of the war when the armies of the Communist Party of China drove the Kuomintang Army out of the mainland to seek refuge in Taiwan.

This disposition of the contending forces did not bring direct conflict between the USA and the Soviet Union, the two recognised superpowers. Nuclear bombs and the missiles to deliver them made war an unacceptable means of settling disputes. While direct conflict no longer made sense as state policy, indirect conflict or wars by proxy, as they came to be called, became the normal way by which one superpower tested the will of the other or sought to gain a strategic advantage, whether real or imagined. Proxy wars were usually, started by one party — usually the Soviet Union introducing a Marxist–Lennist organization in a country and supplying it with weapons to start a revolution. In response the Americans would arm the government of the country, in some instances, the government of a neighbouring country. Conflict would then ensue as has happened in several Central American and African states. Afghanistan was the site of one of these proxy wars; this time America and her allies armed the rebels.

That was broadly the world political background in 1991 when without warning, a series of events brought about the collapse of the Soviet Union. Mikhail Gorbachev, elected as the Union President in 1985, tried to reform the Soviet system by introducing political reforms — more democracy and economic reforms or *perestroika* — movement towards a market economy and away from the rigid centrally planned production system. But he wanted to retain the Communist Party as the leading political force. Gorbachev had little success in *perestroika*.

On 19 August 1991, an attempted *coup* by some of Gorbachev's senior colleagues took place. The *coup* leaders failed to obtain the support of the soldiers or the civilian population. The *coup* collapsed within three days and brought to power Boris Yeltsin, President of the Russian Republic — one of the 15 republics forming the Union.

President Gorbachev was dissatisfied with the Soviet system on two counts. First, the total control of the Soviet media by the Communist Party resulted in concealing unpleasant truths. Modern means of telecommunication and foreign travel revealed to the Soviet people that the outside world was not what their media portrayed. Gorbachev's remedy for this was *glasnost* or openness by granting a degree of independence to media staff as well as allowing public discussion on subjects previously held taboo.

His second target of reform was the economy. It is one of the ironies of the Soviet system of production that while it could produce the most advanced weapons systems not inferior to America's, its performance in producing consumer goods was dismal. What were the reasons? When it came to producing weapons, the purchaser was the Soviet military, which engaged a wide array of scientists and engineers who laid down rigid specifications and had the means to ensure that these were met.

There existed no comparable safeguards to promote quality in consumer goods. In capitalist economies, market competition ensures quality by putting producers and sellers of inferior goods out of business. In the Soviet Union, production of consumer goods was determined by State Planning Commissions; their sales and delivery systems also passed through state controlled channels. Factories' main concern was to ensure that output met planned targets. Experience has shown that not only did quality suffer under this system, but some goods were produced in quantities not wanted by consumers while other goods which consumers wanted remained in short supply. In other words, resources of labour and machinery were not used to the best advantage. Increasingly Soviet economists began to embrace the gospel of market competition and free enterprise, but attempts to reform the economy under Gorbachev were hesitant and generally ineffective.

It was otherwise with *glasnost* and political reform. A new constitution passed in June 1988 provided for an elected assembly of 2,250 representatives, two-thirds by popular vote and one third by "social organisations", the latter to ensure that pro-Communist or at least pro-Gorbachev candidates would form a sizeable group. The elections held on 26 March 1989 could be taken as a landmark event and one of non-confidence in the communist leadership.

Glasnost and democracy had released forces which the Soviet leadership could not control. We must remember that the Soviet Union consisted of 15 republics and the non-Russian republics were hitherto held down by the power of the Russian Army. Given democratic freedom, many of their leaders concluded they should get out of the USSR and function as independent states. While everything was in a state of turmoil, it could hardly be expected that progress through economic reforms could take place. But no one could have foreseen that a group of Gorbachev's colleagues would mount a *coup* in Moscow against him on 19 August 1991. Boris Yeltsin emerged as the strongman playing a leading role in crushing the *coup*. Another effect of the *coup* was that the Communist Party of the Soviet Union virtually ceased to exist. The Central Committee dissolved itself, the Party's branch offices were raided by local authorities and their assets seized. The third effect was that non-Russian republics, beginning with the Ukraine, hurriedly proclaimed their independence.

By December 1991, the Soviet Union had dissolved. The Russian Federation, occupying 76% of the USSR and comprising 51% of its population, remained the most potent force and inherited the seats in international bodies — the UN, World Bank, etc. — formerly occupied by the USSR.

The superpower had disintegrated in a spectacular manner. While the once all-powerful Communist Party that held the USSR together had ceased to exist, no apparatus of government was set up to replace Party control. Economic progress was checkmated without effective implementing agencies. In the end, Yeltsin had to use Army tanks to breakup opposition by some members of the elected Assembly who shut themselves up in the parliamentary building.

We can now turn to our part of the world. I will include only the ASEAN states, the four little dragons — Taiwan, South Korea, Hong Kong and Singapore — and the big dragon, the People's Republic of China. I will leave out Japan, which belongs to the Western industrialised group. In recent years, this area has captured world attention because of continuous high rates of economic growth, far surpassing those of Europe and America.

Consider the growth rates of the ASEAN states in 1993:

Malaysia	8.0%
Thailand	7.9%
Indonesia	6.7%
Philippines	2.3%
Singapore	9.9%

By contrast, the industrialised countries of Europe and America averaged 1.2%. Perhaps a better indication would be the ASEAN states' average annual growth rates over the last five years, 1989–93, to show that last year's performance was no fluke. The simple arithmetic averages are as follows:

Malaysia	8.7%
Thailand	9.4%
Indonesia	8.9%
Philippines	2.0%
Singapore	8.0%

I should add that China's growth rate averaged 9% in the last 15 years, reaching 13.4% last year.

It is only in the last two or three years that the world woke up to the fact that something unusual was happening in our part of the world. Much earlier, the fast growth rates of the four little dragons had aroused extensive academic study in the West but most people did not expect that the countries in South-East Asia would soon follow in their footsteps. These growth rates were much higher than those achieved by developing countries elsewhere, many of whom found it difficult for the economy to keep ahead of population growth, thereby risking a decline in living standards.

One result was the coining of a new phase — the "Pacific Rim countries", a term meant to describe an area of exceptionally fast expansion. In September 1993, the World Bank published a policy research report entitled "The East Asian Miracle" referring to eight countries — Malaysia, Thailand, Indonesia, Singapore, Hong Kong, Taiwan, Korea and Japan. This study gives a detailed analytical inter-country comparison between the eight and other countries in respect of all the important economic variables having a bearing on economic growth.

I will use a different approach from the World Bank study. Instead of discussing economic variables, I want to identify one single condition which made possible the ascent of the four little dragons whose success is historically unprecedented.

Let me, at the outset, explain what I believe to be the real reason for the dragons' ascent. I should tell you that my explanation has not been accepted by the so called neo-classical school of academic economists who maintain that economic growth is the result of savings and investment, the larger the savings and investment, the faster the growth. This theory begs the question: "What causes high rates of savings and investment?" Neo-classical theory has given no satisfactory answer.

In my earlier account of the Industrial Revolution, especially its development in America, what stands out clearly is that the accumulation of wealth resulted from the application of scientific knowledge and production technology to the manufacture of goods and their sale in competitive markets. Successive inventions and their improvements, such as the steam engine, the railway locomotive, the internal combustion engine provided the push to increase investment.

However, the process of extending the benefits throughout the country was a slow one extending over many decades.

We should also note that improvements in scientific knowledge were a slow process and only a small fraction of the population of any country possessed the intellectual capacity to make significant contributions. Nevertheless, scientific knowledge and its technological applications to production accumulated slowly but surely in the universities, research institutions and, later, in Research and Development divisions of Western corporations. There was no short cut for the West.

It was different in post-war Taiwan. In the process of the Cold War, it became a virtual American protectorate. In terms of per capita GNP, it was in 1949 as poor as most developing countries today, certainly poorer at that time than Sri Lanka and the Philippines.

Between 1950 and 1988, no less than 112,659 students left Taiwan to study in overseas universities, mostly in America. More than half of these studied the natural sciences and their applications in various branches of engineering, medicine and agriculture, knowledge of which can be applied to production or health improvements.

What is noteworthy here is that these 112,659 students had direct access to the most advanced knowledge at the time of their study. They did not have to re-invent the wheel. Most of the Taiwanese students remained in the USA and many made notable contributions to America's prosperity. For instance, in 1989, some 20% of the semiconductor engineers in Silicon Valley were Chinese. And there are sufficient numbers of them in the banking and financial business to form the Asian American Financial Association. The number of returned students before 1970 was negligible.

Taiwan's early manufacturing activity consisted of taking advantage of lower wages to produce labour-intensive goods for exports such as textiles, garments, shoes, etc. In 1978, the government decided to change the direction of economic policy.and introduce technology intensive industries. Unlike Singapore, which had to depend on multinational corporations (MNCs), Taiwan decided to depend mainly on her own intellectual resources.

A special effort was mounted to use America's alumni networks to induce the talented to return. Attractive terms were offered in the research institutes which the government had set up. Returning entrepreneurs were offered tax holidays, exemption from custom duties and, in selected areas of high technology, venture capital was offered on generous terms.

By 1988, 19,000 scientists and engineers had returned. These attempts to attract returned students were supplemented by a rapid expansion of tertiary education. In 1952, Taiwan had four universities and four polytechnics. By 1989, Taiwan had 42 universities and 75 polytechnics with an enrolment of 57,247 first degree engineering students and 135,788 polytechnic technicians. In addition, 33,530 students were studying in American universities in the natural sciences and engineering, more than three-quarters at graduate level.

These returned students had the advantage not only of knowledge acquired at American universities but also had many years of experience in working for American corporations. In this way they had extensive knowledge of production technology, management systems and marketing needs. An association of these skills with the industrious lower-paid workers in Taiwan formed a winning combination in any export market. One result of Taiwan's success as an exporter is shown in the foreign exchange reserves she holds, more than US$80 billion, the world's largest.

Taiwan's wage levels are no longer low; in fact, they are higher than Singapore's. Today, like Singapore, she has run out of labour supply. While Singapore arranges to receive guest workers to relieve the shortage, in Taiwan, businessmen go abroad to manufacture products with lower cost workers. Taiwan has been one of the leading foreign investors in Malaysia, Thailand, Indonesia and the Philippines and is now concentrating her attention on mainland China.

One point should be noted in production for export. Taiwan's enterprises have to obtain their inputs of raw materials, components, capital and labour in a free competitive market and they also sell in a free competitive world marker. Neo-classical economists believe — and in this I agree with them — that production conducted in such an environment encourages the best use of economic resources unlike production under a centrally planned economy such as that once operating in the former Soviet Union.

This seems to be the right juncture to discuss mainland China's experience. Deng Xiaoping saw the shortcomings of centrally-planned production earlier than Gorbachev did in the Soviet Union. Unlike Gorbachev, Deng decided to reform only the economy while leaving intact the political system and the administrative apparatus.

Deng had a better grasp than Gorbachev of the essential priorities involved in reforming a Communist state that had existed for several decades. The Communist Party was the glue that held together the institutions governing the huge population of the country. If that glue were to be removed, the whole structure would crumble, as has happened in the former Soviet Union. So, today, China's political system remained intact and largely unchanged from that set up in 1949. The Communist Party of China remains dominant in every sphere of activity. The big decisions on managing the army or running universities are made by leading Party cadres in positions of authority.

I propose to discuss China's economic reforms in three steps — first to explain the nature of the reforms, second to describe their impact on economic growth and, finally, to discuss the present difficulties China finds herself in.

But first I want to tell you about China's level of scientific and engineering knowledge, the prime mover of growth. When the Communist Party of China captured power in 1949, the country was in a miserable state, having experienced unending civil wars since the Qing dynasty fell in 1911 in addition to Japanese invasion since 1931. The Chinese received substantial help from the Soviet Union in four ways. First, the training of scientific and engineering personnel in the USSR; second, the setting up of complete factories in China by Soviet engineers and the training of Chinese personnel to operate these; third, the creation of central planning government departments; fourth, the assistance in setting up universities.

Even after the quarrel between Khrushchev and Mao brought an end to Soviet assistance, the Chinese continued to expand the economy along Soviet lines with state-owned enterprises (SOEs) setting up steel and machinery factories, extracting large reserves of mineral wealth, building new railway networks, new roads, etc. This effort required the services of large numbers of trained personnel. Unlike our neo-classical economists, the Chinese government understood that this production effort required the concurrent expansion of the education system. Today, China's 1,070 universities turn out some 200,000 engineers and 30,000 natural scientists each year.

When he came to power in 1979, Deng realised that China's large capacity to produce goods was not being put to best advantage. He saw the solution in giving greater priority to consumer goods as against heavy industry, in delegating decisions-making authority down to enterprise managements; in reducing the scope of state planning, in liberalising prices of goods and, in general, allowing production to be guided more by the market and less by central planners. All these changes in the economic order were to be carried out in gradual stages. This stands in contrast with Russian economic reforms which, under the advice of foreign academic economists, tried to introduce a completely free market all at once. This is called the "Big Bang" approach and was proved a failure.

The Chinese step-by-step approach produced sustained growth rates at a high but fluctuating level — the so-called "boom and bust" cycle. Nevertheless, standards of living of most people improved markedly under the reforms. The first province to benefit was Guangdong, which was flooded by Hong Kong businessmen who had large orders from Europe and America which they could not fulfil with labour available locally. Some writers claimed that Hong Kong businessmen employed three million workers in factories in China compared with 700,000 in Hong Kong. Other coastal provinces such as Fujian, Jiangsu and Shandong were not slow in following Guangdong's example.

China's troubles are, however, many. To solve the problem of unemployment, SOEs were assigned more workers than they needed. Most are given lifetime employment, virtually free housing, and health care at subsidised rates. Large SOEs provide schools, clinics, hospitals and even universities for employees and their children. Not surprisingly, their losses — made good out of the state budget — are enormous, exceeding the country's defence expenditure.

A politically sensitive issue comes from what China's economists call rent-seeking activities. In plain words, this means taking advantage of your position to make money for yourself. Attempts to stamp it out have not been effective. There is a simple reason for this. While the prices of goods are largely market-determined, the price of labour — wages and salaries — is determined by government regulations. Being a socialist country, workers (or the proletariat, to use Marxist jargon) are the leading class of society and therefore those holding posts of high management responsibility in government and state enterprises cannot get salaries much higher than what workers get. Thus management staff in China are grossly underpaid for the responsibilities they discharge. If we underpay our officials and business managers in this way, "rent-seeking activities" are sure to flourish.

A common belief about the nature of a Communist state with political power concentrated in the hands of a dozen members of the Politburo is that once a major decision is made at the centre, the rest of the country obediently complies. This does not happen in China. There are five tiers of Party and government authority — central, provincial, municipal, county and township. There is a government at each tier; in all, more than 50,000 governments and 50,000 Party committees exist.

This is the main reason why the economy gets out of control from time to time as local governments and Party leaders press ahead with their investment projects beyond the limits set by the Centre. The position is made worse because the Centre lacks the two essential controls over the economy: a tax system under its direct control and a modern banking system with a Central Bank possessing independent powers.

We are now ready to discuss the 21st century; but, first, let me review my main line of analysis. The modern world is a product of European civilisation in creating the scientific method of thinking and enquiry which eventually led to the Industrial Revolution in the 18th century. Nations could get rich by applying science and technology to production. In this way, the age-old causes of war, declared as self-evident by Socrates, had no foundation. Only the Americans seemed to have realised this, but the European states continued to fight each other with fearsome weapons of destruction produced by the scientists.

Amidst the turmoil of the 20th century wars, two Marxist states emerged. One, the Soviet Union has disintegrated in a spectacular way while the other, the People's Republic of China, continues to prosper. But beneath this gloss lies a batch of problems which have remained unsolved for many years and which, if not rectified, can undermine the whole system.

"In the post-war years, four countries achieved fast growth rates for decades mainly by learning modern science and its applications to production. These four have been followed by a further three — Malaysia, Thailand and Indonesia. These have the advantage of abundant natural resources lacking in the four dragons; they have also followed Singapore's example of inviting foreign investors to bring about industrial expansion.

The main influence on the course of events in the 21st century will depend on the outcome of the efforts of the Russian Federation and the People's Republic of China in putting their houses in order. We need not worry about Western Europe. Its present condition of stagnation has many causes, the principal one being overstretching of resources to construct the welfare state. Restructuring the welfare state could be politically difficult but it will have to be done. The Americans, on the other hand, have a greatly more flexible economy but their political system encourages excessive government expenditure, as well as high rates of consumer expenditure, both of which have to be met by borrowing. But America has one great advantage over all other countries, including Japan, in that she attracts talent from all over the world. In the 21st century, this brain power will give America a great competitive advantage over other countries, perhaps a decisive one.

Let us now consider the Russian Federation. Will disintegration continue further? Will wild-eyed nationalists like Vladimir Ehirinovsky take over? Will the contending forces eventually lead to civil war? Or will Boris Yeltsin construct an administrative apparatus which will bring order to the economy with increasing production resulting in rising standards of living? We have seen many examples in the 20th century that rising living standards provide the essential pre-condition of political stability, provided they reach the population in a way seen to be fair.

Nobody knows the answer to these questions. I am inclined to discount the alarmist scenario, partly because I am an optimist by nature. Also I have a great admiration for the Russian people. They have a capacity to bear hardship far exceeding other European people. We must not forget that in terms of scientific knowledge and technology, they are second to none. It is in their applications that their centrally planned system failed to produce results which they, the Russian people, expected. What they have to do is to abandon Karl Marx, follow Adam Smith and introduce the market system to guide production. The Big Bang approach has failed and it is likely that they will try the incremental step-by-step approach the Chinese adopted.

What about the Chinese? Their present troubles can largely be traced to the unreformed state of their political system. The subject of political reform is taboo in China. Perhaps when the last of the Long Marchers have been gathered unto their forefathers, surviving leaders will give serious thought to this subject. I am not suggesting that they should introduce a democratic pluralistic system which the Western media recommend, despite the fact that it was just this attempt by Gorbachev that led to the Soviet Union's disintegration. How the Chinese reform their political system is for them to decide. They know the inner workings of their system in detail and can judge what changes are feasible and what are not.

If contrary to my expectation, both Russia and China fail to make the transition to a market economy and a more open political system, the results could be calamitous for the world. No one could predict what kind of leadership would emerge and whether the leadership could embark on an adventurous foreign policy to strength its hold on the country. There could be a strong temptation to threaten the use of their nuclear arsenal to achieve their objects. Then the 21st century would enter a period of great peril.

I now turn to our part of the world. The World Bank's book *The East Asian Miracle* gave high marks to the policies of the

ASEAN-4 — Malaysia, Thailand, Indonesia and Singapore — over a whole range of economic issues. We can safely expect continued high growth rates, that is, increasing prosperity. But to sustain this growth well into the 21st century the first three countries will have to spend more resources — money and manpower — on education. They have done well in primary education; they need to do more in secondary and tertiary education. In particular, they must try to increase the number of secondary school students studying in the science stream so that there will be sufficient numbers of good quality applicants for the natural sciences and engineering faculties in their universities and polytechnics. This problem is receiving the attention of the three governments and we hope their efforts will meet with early success.

8

What's Gone Wrong in China?*,†

Editors' Note

Written in December 1992 at a time when China was clearly at the crossroads of its next phase of political and economic reform, Goh Keng Swee listed the major political and economic problems China was then facing. Deng Xiaoping, having taken the Nanxun (tour of South China) in February 1992, had by and large won over the ideologues and sceptics that the way forward for China was to further its economic reform. But Deng, still haunted by the collapse of the Soviet Union and Eastern Europe, was wary of the spread of "bourgeois liberalisation", which argued for political reform ahead of economic reform.

The leadership, while going for market reform, was still not abandoning Marxist and Leninist doctrines by upholding the Four Cardinal Principles (the socialist road, the dictatorship of the proletariat, the leadership of the Communist Party, and Marxism-Leninism and Mao Zedong's Thought) as the bottom line for all economic policies. Market reform would look incongruous in such an institutional environment. Hence Goh was able to draw up a long litany of problems and complaints under such a half-reformed economy ranging from China's complicated (lacking clear-cut) central-local

---

*The author wrote this paper in December 1992 under the title "Research Priorities" to guide researchers in IEAPE on their choice of subject matter. On re-reading the paper, the author found the contents very relevant in the light of the difficulties Vice Premier Zhu Rongji's extensive control measures have run into, so this paper was circulated to Ministers and Permanent Secretaries under a different title.
†Published by IEAPE as *IEAPE Commentaries No. 7* on 15 April 1994.

relations to its many inefficient SOEs. He also recommended these problems to be the main research focus of the IEAPE. Looking back, this chapter does carry considerable historical significance.

Abstract: This paper analyses the consequences following from the disparity between China's political system — essentially a Marxist–Leninist state — and her economic system, which is moving rapidly towards an open market economy. The assumption is made that the political system will eventually be reformed to enable China to realise her full economic potential. Under this optimistic scenario, China will reach American living standards in 29 years if she maintains her present rate of economic growth, which has raised per capita GNP by 7.5% a year. A more realistic (but still optimistic) projection would be an annual growth rate of 7.5% for 15 years, 5% after that, and 3% thereafter. China then will arrive at this destination in 2024 AD. The economic parameters are easy to define. China will then produce each year some 450 million tons of steel, 54 million motor vehicles, 27 million refrigerators and 90 million TV sets. She will need some 20,000 universities and polytechnics to produce the educated work force her economy needs. Nobody knows by what path the country can progress from its present mess of contradictory elements to being by far the world's largest economy. It is unclear if some major systemic failure will prevent her ever reaching this objective. This paper tries to identify some of the systemic defects that can frustrate progress, as seen from the present. Although dealing with contemporary problems, the perspective taken is necessarily a long-term one.

In the last twelve years, researchers have focused their attention mainly on China's economic affairs. This holds true of academicians, serious journalism and even of the popular press. Some serious work gets done on political affairs but the effort suffers from a number of drawbacks.

First, reliable information on political processes is hard to come by. Whereas the State Statistical Bureau releases a lot of data on economic variables and numerous conferences — domestic and international — take place on economic issues, what happens at the various levels of the Chinese Communist Party is hidden in a veil of secrecy.

Western scholars who address their minds to political issues have to resort to unusual measures to collect data. Systematic interviews of exiles is one commonly used method, for example by A. Doak Barnett.[1] Reading official documents in search of hidden meanings is another. In the reform era, interviews with ranking government officials can yield some information on specific political issues, but seldom on the inner workings of the Party or state leadership. Recently, Western scholars have written much on the leadership transition, especially after Deng's departure.[2] But nothing comparable to the literature on the Japanese political process has emerged, and is unlikely to emerge because it will be a long time before China's system reaches the state of transparency in Japanese politics.

Why is it necessary to turn our attention to the political system? First, the accounts of Western scholars are unsatisfactory. American scholars often try to apply basic analytical concepts created by their gurus. When applied to political systems which do not operate the American brand of democracy, conclusions can be misleading. Further, Western political science is heavily value-laden, unlike economics. Economists, if they are true to their faith, may avoid value judgements. They deal with measurable variables such as prices, output, employment, wages, etc. These can be high or low, large or small but not good or bad. Other social sciences often get entangled in "normative" concepts: for example, any trend towards democracy is praiseworthy while denial of human rights is reprehensible.

The second reason for a shift of attention from economic to political issues stems from the current state of economic reforms in China. They have only partially fulfilled the hopes and expectations of state and party leaders. While Mr. Deng has recently called for an acceleration of reforms, he has not specified along what direction these reforms should proceed, nor has anybody else. The result is much rhetoric and little substance. This may be a premature judgement if present statements of Deng, Jiang Zemin and others are intended to set the political climate favourable and foreshadow

---

[1] A. Doak Barnett, *Cadres, Bureaucracy, and Political Power in Communist China*, Columbia University Press, 1967.
[2] For example, A. Doak Barnett, *After Deng, What? Will China Follow the USSR?* Washington DC., John Hopkins Foreign Policy Institute, 1991.

unpublished concrete measures now sweeten, held in reserve.[3] This contrasts strongly with the situation in the mid-80s when words were matched by deeds. The State Council issued a stream of regulations, policy statements and directives and launched a series of experimental pilot projects. The Party closely monitored the progress of reforms and took a clear stand in support of reforms, issuing instructions to Party cadres.

The reason for the change between now and the mid-80s can only be partially attributed to the nature of the current and previous Premiers. It is true that Li Peng is cautious by nature while Zhao Ziyang is a risk-taker. But more fundamental causes can be found. In most areas of reform — prices, enterprise management, decentralisation of political authority, reduction of central control over allocation of resources — numerous vexatious difficulties have emerged. The solutions in purely economic terms are not difficult to find and China's leaders do not need foreign experts to tell them what to do.

The Chairman of the People's Bank of China, China's Central Bank, described the situation succinctly to Dr. Richard Hu and Mr. Koh Beng Seng when the two recently visited Beijing. "We know what's wrong with the banking system," he said. "Furthermore we know what to do to correct the faults. The trouble is what we have to do may create difficulties greater than what we now face. Therefore we do nothing." We shall return to this subject later as the paralysis that has seized their banking system is illustrative of what one may call "problems of system interface". All that need to be said at this stage is that economic reforms in other areas are heading for a similar dead end.

What does "system interface" mean and how does it work? In China, as elsewhere, we can conceptualise the working of the whole society in terms of the political system and the economic system. To further simplify this complex subject, the former can be considered

---

[3] It is difficult to believe, for instance, that the torrent of official and research literature on the benefits of extending the shareholding system to Chinese enterprises is based on a sound grasp of economic principles. Nobody has pointed out that until China has in operation a standard system of modern accounting, the proliferation of shareholding units must lead to disputes, particularly as China has no company law today.

as consisting of all institutions connected with the exercise of authority at all levels of society — from the President, Prime Minister and Chief of the General Staff to the village police chief. The economic system consists of the institutions concerned with the production and marketing of goods and services. They include factories, finance, commerce, transportation, mining, construction enterprises as well as state-supplied infrastructure. "Institutions" mean not only identifiable agencies such as government departments, political parties and business enterprises, but also laws and customary methods of working and the belief system underlying these. In China, there is the added complication of the Communist Party of China (CPC). The CPC, like other Marxist parties, holds the monopoly of power. In addition, it claims to be the sole source of truth. Despite great blunders like the Great Leap Forward and the Cultural Revolution, and constant revision of what the truth is, it has not abandoned this claim. Political control rests on the Four Cardinal Principles which can be reduced to one — the CPC shall always exercise a monopoly of power. Having said this, one must also admit that it is difficult to imagine how a pluralist system can operate in China in the foreseeable future.

With this meaning of "system" we can quickly identify the source of the "dead end" problem that economic reforms have run into. The two systems in China are basically incompatible. On a Marxist political system has been superimposed economic reforms that increasingly make use of market-type business transactions. At the same time, state-owned enterprises (SOEs) dominate major "strategic" sectors. This falls in line with Marxist dogma and results naturally from the command economy which China established from 1949 onwards. Let us briefly digress on the Soviet experience to explain the role played by "system interface".

In the former Soviet Union, the command system quickly raised industrial production to great heights in the 1930s, and during World War II produced sufficient weapons to defeat Hitler's armies. After the war, the industrial system produced strategic weapons as fearsome as the American's and this propelled the Soviet Union to super-power status. This was no mean achievement. It was made possible because the political and economic systems were compatible with each other in the production of weapons and there was no trouble in the system interface. The State was both producer and consumer. As producer, the State could allocate the best brains and sufficient material resources to meet military needs. As a consumer, the State could assign scientists and general staff experts to maintain high quality standards.

But what the command system could not do was to produce consumer goods in the volume, variety and quality which European and American consumers enjoyed. Consumers have to take what the State produces, and state enterprises have no incentive to meet consumer demand in the way producers in market economies have to do. Producers in market (capitalist) economies literally engage in a life-and-death competitive struggle. Success brings large fortunes, failure bankruptcy. Hence, enterprise attracts the best talent in the country and competition between them ensures that costs are trimmed to the minimum and products are what consumers want. Competition also results in an unceasing flow of product and process innovation.

The political system in Marxist states is prevented from using the free market enterprise system, since the dogma claims that this will lead to economic anarchy. So they have set up a structure of monopolistic state enterprises directed by the Central Planning authority. Enterprise managers' incentives are governed by their ability to meet planning quotas, regardless of whether consumer demand is adequately met. In the end, this proves the system's undoing. When Soviet citizens came to know of the disparity of living standards (necessarily measured in terms of consumer goods), faith in the system declined, and when Gorbachev's attempts at "glasnost" and "perestroika" failed, the result was a spectacular collapse of the system which none of the experts had predicted.

The question that springs to the mind is: "Does the same fate await China?" No one knows the answer with certainty, nor is it useful to assemble the arguments for and against a collapse. What we know is that China has made progress in "perestroika" but has stood firmly against "glasnost". "Perestroika" involves changes to the economic structure while "glasnost" must lead to changes to the political system. Chinese resolve to resist political change has doubtless been strengthened by the sudden unravelling of the Soviet system. Another element is that no one — either inside or outside China — claims to know how to set about political reforms, other than naive pro-democracy ideologues in the West who believe a pluralistic political structure will solve all of China's problems. Whatever the ultimate answer turns out to be, political reforms will be a long and continuing process. Furthermore, there are no precedents to guide China's leaders in their search for political reforms. Among China's think tanks, the subject is now taboo. It takes a dissident writing from abroad to say, "... people hope that Deng's ideas and policies about deepening reform can also penetrate areas including politics and ideology."[4] Yet as the Chinese leaders eventually realise that their economic reforms have got stuck in a political morass of their own making, they will pay greater attention to political reforms. When this moment of truth arrives, what will they do?

We cannot be sure. Political reforms mean different things to different people. They may concern small changes to institutions or current practices. Here we are concerned with fundamental changes which will transform the present Marxist–Leninist system into one which maximises the economic potential that China possesses. We can approach the subject in one of the two ways. The first is to consider the political institutions which all modern industrial states have. These include a legal system of which an independent judiciary is an essential element, a professional civil service, a participatory system of leadership selection, an open information system, and a constitution, written or otherwise, which sets out the limits of authority of main components of the political structure. There are large variations between modern states in the structure and functioning of these institutions. Yet it is possible to see some similarities in the purpose and mission of these institutions, whether they are universities, central banks or legislatures. So one approach could be that the political institutions of China should be reformed in the direction of those found in the US, Europe and Japan.

---

[4]Xu Jiatun, "The Best of Capitalism Can Stop the Collapse of Communism", *South China Morning Post*, 1 June 1992.

This approach suffers from two weaknesses. First, since Chinese leaders of all hues and persuasions have set their minds against "bourgeois liberalisation" (which is what this exercise amounts to), a political reform programme of this kind cannot get started unless the Party renounces its Marxist doctrines. Since these doctrines constitute the leaders' source of legitimacy, renunciation is unlikely to happen. However, as we shall argue later, there could be indirect ways by which the present limitless (in theory) Party authority can be constrained.

Suppose that the intent of copying Western institutions can be disguised, the second weakness reveals itself. Where to start? How to justify changes in terms acceptable to and understood by leaders, cadres and masses? What should be the sequence of reforms so that action in one area reinforces the efficiency in other areas? On the basis of present knowledge we can find no satisfactory answers to these questions and therefore we should try another approach.

This approach can start with a study of individual items of economic reform and search for the reasons for the state of immobility to which they have been reduced. We shall choose only two items — reforms of the management of SOEs and the growth of widespread corruption. Corruption has been included here because its eruption is a direct consequence of economic reforms and illustrates clearly the failure of the interface between the political and economic systems. Both these issues will have a serious effect on the political fortunes of future leaders. The erosion of legitimacy of the regime depends crucially on these two issues. Hitherto the regime can surmount threats to their legitimacy, first, because of the fast increases of living standards since the reforms began and second, the legendary authority of the first generation of revolutionary leaders.

Scholars are in agreement that the successor leadership will lack the authority of the old guard.[5] They may get by for a while if the economy performs as well as it did in the past decade. There is no guarantee that, even if long-term trends are favourable, there will not be setbacks,

---

[5] A. Doak Barnett (1991) *op.cit.* Barnett believes that the succession will probably take place in an orderly way as rivals for top posts will not take their differences in the open. Under this scenario, the army will not intervene in the succession process.

such as what happened in 1988–89. Should public discontent on the scale of those years recur, it is unlikely that the successor leaders can resort to the repressive measures of the Tiananmen Incident. A situation may well develop, familiar in many Third World countries, in which political instability and economic deterioration feed on each other. The position in China is made especially sensitive and the leadership's legitimacy vulnerable because of the extensive scale on which graft and corruption take place. Corruption will be tolerated and discontent eased so long as continuous fast economic growth takes place. But the sharp business cycles experienced by China's economy can introduce a destabilizing element during a prolonged downturn.

Under the present interface of the political and economic systems, corruption has assumed endemic proportions. Corruption can be traced to two causes. The incomplete state of economic reforms has enlarged opportunities for corruption. The two-tiered pricing system — featuring controlled prices for privileged buyers and market prices for the others — has been frequently cited as creating such opportunities. At the same time, the low pay of management staff, a result of socialist egalitarian dogma, has increased the temptation to seize these opportunities. Resorting to drastic action, such as public executions of culprits, has failed to stem the tide. An important factor contributing to this outcome can be found in the institutional practices authorised under the political set-up. The principle of Party supremacy in all matters prevents police investigations from dealing with suspects if these are cadres above a certain rank. The police have to negotiate with the Party before they can proceed. The frustrations and miseries suffered by the police from this and other sources are graphically described in a recent article "End Criminals' Sway Over Public Security", Annex A.[6]

---

[6]The article first appeared in *People's Public Security News*, 27 June 1992 and was republished in *Inside China Mainland*, September 1992. The risks of the uncontrollable increase of corruption, as experienced in the last years of the Kuomintang, can be exaggerated. The Party's Disciplinary Commission is by no means ineffective. The top leaders observe high standards of conduct even though their close relations are suspected of influence-peddling.

It is only if the Party — and Party leaders — are not placed above the law that measures to stamp out corruption can be effective. A necessary condition for this is a major reform of the political system and this in turn requires a change in the mindset of China's leaders for which there is little evidence. This subject will be discussed in later paragraphs.

We now turn to management reforms of SOEs. It is not for want of physical, manpower and financial resources that reforms have stalled. SOEs have been allotted the most talented engineers and managers, given preferential access to raw materials, energy, modern imported industrial equipment and transportation, and the finance and foreign exchange to buy these. Yet they have performed badly. The reasons for poor performance have been the subject of innumerable studies, conferences, speeches and party and government directives. In May this year, an International Conference on "Improving the Performance of State-Owned Industrial Enterprises" was held in Beijing's State Guesthouse. The Vice Minister of the Production Office under the State Council delivered a paper titled "The Way to Deepen China's Reform for Greater Economic Returns by State-Owned Industrial Enterprises". This paper, as well as the others, is notable for a lack of fresh ideas.

Equally innumerable are the proposed remedies.[7] In the meantime, deterioration of SOE performance continues unabated, resulting in increasing state subsidies which in turn lead to increasing budget deficits.[8] Chinese leaders have expressed their displeasure over this on

---

[7] Goh Keng Swee, "Li Peng on China's State Enterprises", *IEAP Discussion Paper No. 14*, 21 December 1991 and Yang Mu, unpublished IEAPE paper, "Reforming State-Owned Enterprises in China".

[8] This topic, as expected, drew sustained attention among China's officials and research institute scholars. Former Finance Minister Wang Bingqian can hardly avoid a reference to this subject in his annual budget statements. References to this obstinate difficulty appear in several IEAPE papers. Among these are Goh Keng Swee, "Decision of the Central Committee of the Chinese Communist Party on Economic Policy, 9 November 1989"; (*IEAP Discussion Paper*, 21 May 1991); Eu Chooi Yip, "Chinese Reformers Regain the High Ground" (*IEAP Discussion Paper No. 5*, 7 June 1991); Zou Ziying, "Debt Chains in China" (*IEAP Background Brief No. 20*, 5 December 1991); Eu Chooi Yip, "The Contract Responsibility System in Chinese State Enterprises: A Flawed Device" (*IEAP Background Brief No. 23*, 20 January 1992).

numerous occasions. Those remedies that they have applied have proved ineffective. After the Tiananmen Incident the Party adopted the hardline approach of recentralisation in 1989. It only worsened the matter.[9] Official admission of the impasse has been made in a series of three recent articles in *Jingji Ribao* summarized in the *China Economic News*, 7 September 1992 (see Annex B).[10]

The State has shrunk from taking effective action which must take the form of immediate restructuring of at least a third of the SOEs. The reason is simply that millions of redundant workers and staff members would lose their jobs. The World Bank puts the situation bluntly "... it is unrealistic to expect hard budgets, implying possible bankruptcies and unemployment, as long as SOEs workers (over 100 million, largely concentrated in urban centres) continue to be dependant upon their workplace for housing and pensions, in the absence of socialized unemployment compensation".[11] Since unemployment compensation schemes are poorly structured and more poorly managed, these millions will create social discontent of a magnitude the leaders dare not face. Yet temporising would not resolve the problem and merely ensures that the dislocation will be greater if remedies are postponed even longer.

Behind this lack of political will to address SOE management reforms, which is perhaps the most serious economic trouble China is facing, is the State's inability to construct a reliable mechanism to pay unemployment benefits. This is not a difficult matter and many countries have such schemes in force. Why has China been unable to do so?

The Centre does not pass laws and regulations to set up unemployment compensation agencies throughout China, binding on them in all details of operational and financial procedures. Nor does the centre set up a nation-wide agency under its direct control, as is done in other modern states. Instead, in recognition of regional

---

[9] Goh Keng Swee, 21 May 1991, *op.cit.*

[10] There is no reason to believe that the unspecified measures promised in the article, to be revealed after the 12 October 1992 Party Congress, will fare better than their predecessors.

[11] JBRD, *Country Briefs*, 6 July 1992, p. 545.

variations in China, only general guidelines are issued by the central government. These are elaborated on by the provincial governments which may set up social security agencies to serve employees and enterprises under their jurisdiction. The main implementing agencies are local authorities — cities and counties — who assign the work to their labour bureaus or set up labour service companies operating under the labour bureaus. Evidence in the literature indicates that workers who lose their jobs find it extremely difficult to get unemployment benefits. This is hardly surprising. Payments to the fund come to only 1% of a worker's standard pay, i.e. excluding bonus. According to an authoritative estimate, this is sufficient to serve only 600,000 unemployed workers. The potential number of unemployed, that is, surplus workers employed in SOEs comes to 20 million.[12]

This inability to set up and manage a nation-wide agency is not confined to social security measures like unemployment insurance. In a crucial field such as central banking, problems of relation between centre, provinces and localities pose insoluble difficulties. The People's Bank of China (PBOC) has 30 provincial branches whose staffs answer both to the provincial governments and Beijing's PBOC. As their payroll comes from the provincial government, there is little doubt who has the bigger influence in normal circumstances. When the provincial PBOC resists a request for easy money in deference to directives from the centre, the clinching argument is used against the staff, "Your family lives in our house, eats our food and drinks our water. How can you refuse to help us?[13]

There must be several strong institutional and political and cultural reasons why the Chinese cannot get away from this system. IEAPE papers referred to earlier explained how the system works but did not discuss why other forms of organisation could not have been installed.

---

[12] Li Yuan (Director, State Commission for Restructuring the Economic System), "Boosting the Reform of the Social Security System", paper presented to the International Conference on "Improving the Performance of State-Owned Industrial Enterprises in China", 4–6 May 1992.

[13] In 1989 I was told in Beijing that the Chairman of the Sichuan PBOC committed suicide because he could not resolve this conflict of loyalties.

China's constitution has undergone five revisions. The present, passed in 1982, like previous editions, describes the institutions of the central government — the State — and its relations with citizens. Provincial authority is defined in a general way in the 1982 Constitution in Articles 104, 107 and 108. This allows provincial party and government institutions to replicate the institutions at the centre and follow their procedures. Similarly, cities follow the provincial example, though not all departments of provincial government are set up at city and lower levels.

One would expect that the laws, regulations and directives of the centre are binding on lower levels. Thus power is highly centralised. The exercise of central authority may be looked at from two angles: first, the negative or prohibitive commands; second, the positive or affirmative directives. As examples of the prohibitive commands, provincial governments are not allowed to enter into air traffic agreements with foreign airlines, this right being reserved by the centre. Another example is that until recently business enterprises of any category cannot take part in foreign trade unless expressly sanctioned by the centre.

In general, the writ of central prohibitions runs through the country, though it is not unknown for provincial governments or even local authorities to approve certain requests made by foreign investors for which they have no authority to do, much to the chagrin of the foreign investors when these agreements are annulled.[14] The trouble with the effectiveness of prohibitions is that it induces lack of initiative down the hierarchy.

The central leadership understood this and hence from time to time put forward schemes of decentralisation of authority. The earliest such exercise took place during the Great Leap Forward in 1959,

---

[14]Sembawang Aviation, a Singapore SOE, received permission from the provincial government of Hainan to set up a JV airline to serve tourists travelling between Haikou (the capital) and Sanya (a tourist hot spot), an eight-hour journey by road. The company also received permission to fly 14-seater Cessnas. On the arrival of the Cessnas at Haikou early in 1992, the company was told by a Beijing Aviation Authority official that the Hainan government had no authority to form the JV company and the Cessnas have not been approved for flying in China.

with disastrous results. The Cultural Revolution was partially inspired by the rigidities of central bureaucratic controls and produced even greater disasters. The economic reforms introduced since 1979 required by their nature extensive delegation of authority. This delegation is effected by the withdrawal of previous items of prohibition as well as the introduction of new rights to provincial and local authorities to enterprises. However, the lack of precise demarcation of authority resulted in unending tussles between the centre and provinces. The root of the troubles can be traced directly to China's centralised constitutional arrangements.

Despite all these shortcomings, the reforms have been spectacularly successful, benefiting not only the coastal provinces most affected by them but also the inner provinces. The average annual growth rates of China's GDP since 1979 have exceeded that of Singapore's. Professor Lawrence H. Summers, Chief Economist of the World Bank, predicts that if present growth trends persist, by the year 2003, China's economy would be as large as the US and thereafter overtake her by rapid strides.[15] This may come as a surprise to those accustomed to read conventional estimates of China's per capita GNP as US$350, ranking her with countries like Pakistan. Such estimates do not take into account purchasing power adjusted rates of exchange. Prices of most goods and services converted into, say, Singapore dollars at the current rate of exchange, are extremely low. For international comparisons of GNP, differences in purchasing power should be taken into account.[16]

However, it is unlikely that Professor Summers' projections will be fulfilled unless the Chinese leadership finds solutions to the increasingly intractable difficulties that economic reforms are encountering, of which we referred to two important examples. Our

---

[15] Lawrence H. Summers, "The Economics of the 1990s: Back to the Future", *The International Economy*, July/August 1992. Annexes C and D give the graphs used by Summers. The present GDP of China has already exceeded that of Japan.

[16] See John Wong, "What Is China's Per-Capita GNP?", *IEAP Background Brief, No. 18*, 18 October 1991.

conclusion is that they will be unable to do so without addressing needed reforms in the political system.[17]

When the centre affirms a new policy or some amendment to an existing policy, it can be sure of effective implementation only in ministries and enterprises under its direct control and even so only under certain limitations. Where the subject concerns several ministries, implementation can run into difficulties over inter-ministerial co-ordination.[18] This problem exists elsewhere as inter-departmental "turf battles" are not unknown. It is when the scene of action moves to provinces and cities that unique Chinese characteristics make their appearance. There are more than 2,000 government and Party centres of authority in the provinces, cities and counties. Each of these, we noted, replicate the organisational structure of the centre. The result is a huge bureaucratic maze operating on dual lines of control by both Party and government.

One outcome of this constitutional arrangement is that decisions reached between centre and province, and between province and lower levels generally result from negotiation between upper and lower levels of authority. The sharing of taxation provides an outstanding example. China has no national revenue collection agency apart from customs duties which yield 5% of total state revenue. The centre legislates what taxes are to be raised throughout the country, setting out rates of taxes and details of tax liability. The collection is done by provinces and localities using personnel employed by them. The sharing of tax proceeds varies from one tax to another, from one province to another, and all agreements reached through negotiation. According to the World Bank, no less than six systems of revenue sharing between centre and provinces are in

---

[17] In a seminar I gave at Johns Hopkins University in August 1992, I was assured that the Chinese will overcome these problems their own way and in good time. They have shown a genius for getting out of scrapes in ways no foreigner can predict.

[18] Kenneth Lieberthal and Michel Oksenberg, "Understanding China's Bureaucracy", *China Business Review*, Nov–Dec 1986, gives a good short account. The literature on the subject is enormous both from scholars, journalists and businessmen.

operation.[19] These systems are subject to constant revision when the centre deems it necessary. For instance, Guangdong delivers an agreed amount in the base year with a percentage increase each year. It keeps the balance. The Guangdong government is effectively a tax farmer of Beijing. In return for a high percentage retention of revenues collected, Guangdong does not receive funds for expenditure on infrastructure development as do other provinces.

Although tax-levying authority rests with the centre, it is not unknown for localities to levy their own taxes or fees under all kinds of pretext. The proceeds of these imposts are not shared with anybody. The centre regularly rails against this practice to no effect.

It is clear from the foregoing that the weaknesses we described earlier are rooted in the constitutional provision and practices between the centre, provinces and localities. Provinces need to have written constitutions in the same way as large countries as the USA, India, Canada and others do. The limits between central and provincial authority need to be precisely defined. When these limits are breached by one party or the other, a third party is needed to adjudicate. In countries with written constitutions and several layers of authority, disputes are referred to the law courts. But this cannot be done in China unless a modern legal system is established.

There are, however, major obstacles to setting up such a system in China. First, the ideology of Marxism–Leninism regards the legal system as the instrument by which the ruling class maintains its authority by suppressing the antagonistic lower class. In capitalist countries, the system includes, in addition to law courts, the police, prisons and ultimately the army as instruments through which the bourgeoisie prevent a proletariat uprising. However, in a socialist state, where the workers have (or are supposed to have) turned the tables on the bourgeoisie, the legal system's function is to keep their former oppressors down until a classless society eventually emerges, whereupon the state (including the government and the legal system) withers away, there being no need to oppress anybody.

---

[19] Ramgopal Agarwala, "China: Reforming Intergovernmental Fiscal Relations", *World Bank Discussion Papers No. 178*, China and Mongolia Department.

Until that happy event arrives, the Party must safeguard the Revolution. In this crucial role, it cannot allow any institution to supercede its authority. That is to say, the judiciary must be subject to party control and indeed the Chief Justice of China, a chemical engineer by training, urged that "courts at all levels must self-consciously follow party leadership, and judges and other judicial cadres must abide by the policies of the Party".[20]

In recent years, there has been encouraging evidence that several of the leading jurists in China are dissatisfied with the legal system and have been engaged in revising the accepted Marxist theory of law. The difficulty here stems from the division of jurists into two camps — the legal scholar, mainly law professors in leading universities, and judicial personnel, those manning judicial posts ranging from the heads of county or village courts to the Chief Justice. Law professors do not have the same access to the leadership as have, for instance, economists. They have to overcome two obstacles — first, to win acceptance within academic circles of their viewpoint; second, to convince the Party leadership. So far the second objective remains in the distance but some progress has been made in securing academic respectability.[21] The arguments used can be exceptionally doctrinairian. For instance, the term "citizens" is to be preferred to "people" in a socialist society. "People" is counterpoised to "enemy of the people" to whom equality before the law cannot be extended whereas the term "citizen" is politically neutral.

The arguments used do not concern us here, but what is significant is their rejection of the Russian doctrine of socialist legality. This is a necessary first step to building the intellectual infrastructure upon which a modern legal system must rest. The position of legal reform differs from political reform where the leaders set the tune and determine the pace. So far as intellectual theorising on political reforms goes, the position is a total shamble, with "liberal extremists"

---

[20]Wu Xieying, "The Role of Law in China's Open Door Policy (Part II)", *IEAPE Background Brief No. 35*, 29 June 1992.

[21]See Carlos W. H. Lo, "Rejecting the Traditional Socialist Theory of Law", *China Information*, Vol. VII, No. 1, Summer 1992.

and "diehard conservatives" engaged in a dialogue of the deaf. The liberal camp was led not by a scholar trained in political science but an astro-physicist, Professor Fang Lizhi. The liberals demand no less than the abolition of the monopoly of power enjoyed by the CPC. There is, however, an intermediate school consisting mainly of law professors in various universities.[22] These accept the Four Cardinal Principles but assert that the party itself must act in a lawful way.

There is another even more formidable obstacle arising from Chinese history and culture. Chinese people the world over, other than those trained in Western law, do not have the concept of law as exerting transcendental influence over the whole of society, including government and government leaders. Joseph Needham contrasted Western attitudes towards law with Chinese attitudes and traced the origin of these attitudes to cultural differences in the early ages of development of each civilisation. Western civilisation owes much to Greco-Roman political philosophies and legal theories. The Romans, because of the diversity of nationalities in Europe, found it necessary to introduce the concept of natural justice to override the customary laws of each nationality. The Chinese, on the other hand, being culturally homogenous, found no necessity to do this.[23]

The leadership are aware that their present legal practices constitute a major hindrance to the inflow of foreign direct investment. To improve the investment environment, the State Council has introduced a large volume of economic legislation, in order to clarify the legal position on contracts, trademarks, intellectual property, joint ventures, etc. Special attention has been paid to the rights of foreign partners in joint ventures or wholly-owned enterprises. While this has improved matters, little has been done to ensure that when disputes reach the courts, settlements are fair and when damages are awarded, they are paid.

---

[22] See Wu Xieying, unpublished IEAPE paper, "Debate in China's Constitutional Amendment: the Major Schools of Thought", August 1992.

[23] Joseph Needham (ed.), *Sciences & Civilisation in China*, Cambridge University Press, 1989, Ch. 18 "*Human Law and the Laws of Nature in China and the West*", pp. 518–583.

Because of uncertainty over legal processes in business disputes, foreign parties try to avoid the law courts and follow the Chinese custom of pulling *guanxi* as the preferred mode of obtaining redress. This subject is widely discussed in foreign journals specialising in China's business and the general atmosphere created is detrimental to direct investment from Western and Japanese enterprises. However, Taiwan, Hong Kong and, to a less extent, Singapore businessmen do not find China's method of settlement of business disputes a disincentive.

Apart from pressure from Western multi-national corporations to improve the legal system, China will be increasingly exposed to pressure from Western countries, especially the US, that Chinese enterprises observe the various commitments which their government have entered into, for example, on property rights, and where they do not, redress can be obtained throught expeditious enforcement in their law courts. The present situation is a response to specific pressure in particular cases, which is cumbersome and unsatisfactory. Western enterprises operating in China want legal redress of infringements to be made as a matter of course through the law courts as is done in modern industrial states. At present, aggrieved Western enterprises must make a convincing case to their embassy in Beijing. Embassies of large countries like the US, Japan and Germany know where and how to bring effective pressure to bear. This is a time-consuming process. Further, such a method of redress is not available to investors from small countries like Singapore, who prefer to nurse their wounds quietly as they believe that reference to our embassy in Beijing will not bring any benefits.

While the legal system has been found inadequate in meeting the needs of foreign investors and China's trading partners, it has not done too badly in its dealings with China's society as a whole, especially the tradition-bound rural society. Communist cadres appointed to judicial positions have simplified procedures and made laws more comprehensible to ordinary people. Where population movements are much restrained and people have to live with those with whom they have disputes, settlement by compromise has advantages over legal suits in the Western style.[24] Because of the large number of untrained judges that have to be appointed, miscarriage of justice can easily occur in the vast stretches of the rural areas. Hence it is no bad thing for the Party to exercise some supervision over court judgements. Some of the judgements had to be written by a primary school teacher because the judge was presumably illiterate.[25] We can see that reforms of China's legal system are not an undertaking that can be lightly entered into.

We are now in a position to identify areas of research priorities. A small institute like the IEAPE with limited resources of finance and manpower must focus its attention on a few small areas. Ranging over the vast areas of the Chinese economy and political system would waste what little resources we have. We can classify our areas of interest according to the short-term or longer-term perspective. Most of the items listed below fall in the field of economic reform. The reason is that a direct investigation into the political system in its upper reaches (where the big decisions are made) will yield little useful result unless the researcher enjoys the confidence of the top leaders and has constant access to them. This devoutly-wished condition hardly ever exists in the real world. Focusing attention on economic reforms can bring to light the perceptions of the leadership on the directions and scope of political reforms that have to be made to improve the interface between the political and economic systems.

In the short-term, the following subjects are of interest: .

(i) Progress achieved in the management reforms of SOEs, in particular, the impact of the recently promulgated Enterprise Law. This study can produce evidence to support or falsify the opinion expressed here that these reforms have entered a blind alley.

---

[24]Victor H. Li, "The Evolution and Development of the Chinese Legal System" in John M. H. Lindbeck (ed.), *China: Management of a Revolutionary Society*, University of Washington Press, 1971.
[25]Hikota Koguchi, "Some Observations about Judicial Independence in Post-Mao China", in R. H. Folsom & J. H. Minan (eds.), *Law in the People's Republic of China*, Kluwer Academic Publishers, Dordrecht, 1989.

(ii) Progress of price reforms. This subject has been excluded fromconsideration in earlier paragraphs, not because it is unimportant but because of its technical complexity. Some of the leading reform economists that support price reforms also claim that market prices should operate within the ambit of a centrally-planned economy. The exact meaning is unclear as their statements are usually made in normative and not analytical terms. One can only sympathise with the view of Professor Wu Jinglian and Dr. Zhou Xiaochuan who pointed out that much of China's troubles originated in attempts to combine these two irreconcilable elements.[26] No coherent long-term economic policy could emerge from this combination. Study of price reforms must take note of the questionable accuracy of some of the statements made on the subject.[27] Such public statements may lead one to the conclusion that the most difficult part of price reform has already been carried out. In fact the most crucial areas — energy, minerals and industrial raw materials, rail and air transportation — have been considered too important for price liberalization beyond close limits. However the 14th Congress, which has introducing a new concept of "socialist market economy" to replace the "socialist commodity economy", may portend a more determined effort at freeing all prices.

The most critical items to watch are those relating to energy. A recent news item states that SOEs engaged in oil and coal production sustain losses which amount to 42% of total SOEs losses.[28] If true, this raises several questions. Why have prices not

---

[26] The subject of price reform and resource allocation through the market mechanism is extensively discussed in Robert C. Hsu, *Economic Theories in China, 1979–88,* Cambridge University Press, 1991.

[27] For instance, a recent news report claims that the prices of most agricultural products have been decontrolled. If "most" refers to variety, this is correct. If we list out various farm produce, i.e. different varieties of vegetables, flowers, herbs, etc. the prices of most of these are free of control. However, if we take into account value of output, the claim is false. Grain, cotton, edible oil, remain under price control and they account for probably 90% of farm products excluding livestock.

[28] Xinhua News Agency, *Collected Internal References No. 14,* August 1992, pp. 9–12.

been raised to realistic levels to eliminate a large part of the state's intractable problem? Bearing in mind that these prices are way below world prices — ex-pithead coal prices come to around 15% of international prices — the need for a remedial action is both urgent and obvious.

(iii) The banking and financial system needs close monitoring. Though some changes have been made, the essential role of the system remains as the government's cashier. This has exposed the economy to severe bouts of the business cycle experienced since 1979. The banking system cannot be transformed into independent commercial units until price liberalization, especially prices of "essential" commodities and services, has progressed much further. If bank loans were to be based on the credit worthiness of borrowers, SOEs in the coal, oil and raw material industries will be starved of capital.

(iv) Monitor the progress of China's reform-minded jurists, especially their impact on the thinking of members of the younger leaders. Absence of impact need not be a cause for discouragement as younger leaders do not voice what may be regarded as dissenting opinions, especially on sensitive political issues. We should also follow statements of eminent leaders to note if they contain more than previous conventional exhortations about "socialist legality". Meanwhile we should deepen our understanding of China's legal system.

(v) Begin more intensive studies of provincial administrations, especially in areas where direct investment from Singapore is likely to take place. This study will throw more reliable and concrete information on how relations between the centre and provinces are regulated.

(vi) Begin a study of selected city administrations. IEAPE has been unsuccessful in trying to get details of city budgets. It is absurd that information of this kind cannot be easily obtained, but that seems to be the position.

(vii) Miscellaneous items. One group can be regarded as economic aberrations. This includes regional blockades resulting in fragmentation of the large domestic market. The literature, Chinese as well as Western (including World Bank and IMF studies) make constant reference to this subject. Anecdotal evidence supports the view that blockades are in widespread, if irregular, use. However there has been an absence of particular details such as which province is blockading what goods. One result of economic reforms has been the elimination of trade monopolies and the proliferation of trade channels in domestic commerce. Is it possible to enforce blockades given the porous state of inter-provincial transport and trade links? If blockades no longer pose a significant issue, why does the literature continue to pay attention to it? Does it indicate a propensity among scholars to accept popular notions without looking for hard evidence of their authenticity? Another issue is the low pay of intellectuals working in government agencies, universities and research institutes and management staff of SOEs. A third refers to welfare functions performed by SOEs such as subsidised housing, old age pensions, etc. We can also include the poor standards of accounting here. These are termed aberrations because they are so obviously discordant that remedies should not be long in coming, nor are the remedies too difficult to apply, except for the welfare functions of state enterprises.

The second group consists of favoured policy measures, the efficacy of which are uncertain. This group includes the widespread adoption of the shareholding system, the establishment of stock markets and mergers of SOEs into large holding companies. It is possible that unexpected benefits may occur one day.

For part of the research, especially on the first three subjects, reliance on documentary material will form a significant part of the effort. We can supplement this effort by inviting scholars and officials from China on visiting fellowships or study visits. Such invitations must not be made on impulse but after careful examination and weighing of alternatives. In addition, we should tap the experience of Singaporean investors in China. Hitherto these have been secretive, so much so that our Embassy in Beijing does not keep records of their existence. Lists of Singaporean direct investors were provided by the State Council's Special Economic Zone office and this list would omit investments made outside the zone. Yong Pow Ang's researches on a sample of investors reveal a widespread disinclination to discuss their experience. With the establishment of the East Asian Consultancy Company, relations in future should be better. It should then be possible to collect systematic information on the subject.

From a long-term perspective, the dominant issue will be political reforms. Under the present political climate, it is unlikely that any discussion of significance will take place in China and this may continue until the last of the "eight immortals" has departed from the political scene. The first sign of impending change will be a stirring of interest in academic circles on some aspect of political reform. Such incursions into apparently forbidden territory can only be made under the protection and encouragement of someone in high authority. Or an eminent leader may express some forceful views about the need for political reforms which embolden research institutes to embark on serious studies. All that can be done now is to watch for the appearance of these hopeful signs. In China, substantial changes in policy are usually heralded by intellectual activity sponsored in this way.

As leaders often herald intellectual innovation among scholars, a watch should be kept of leadership changes. The strengthening of technocratic leaders is bound to discourage the kind of obscuralist dogmatism dominant before 1979 and by no means absent today. We should also pay attention to agents of change which have been increasingly forceful in recent years, such as townships and village enterprises and the private economy. Several reforms sanctioned by the State Council have their origins in provinces and localities, for instance the abolition of the Advisory Council. Another institution worth monitoring is grassroots elections of party leaders. If liberal ideas were to take root, this could be the starting point.

Goh Keng Swee
7 December 1992

ANNEX A

End Criminals' Sway Over Public Security

People's Public Security News (人民公安报)
Beijing, 27 June 1992

Anti-crime Measures Ineffective

Recently, this reporter has heard a number of comrades relate that there are still those having difficulty striking back against criminal activities. I find that the symptoms and causes of this ineffectiveness are as follows:

1. Appeals from acquaintances, relatives. Quite a few cadre police have reacted strongly to this, saying that now whenever they handle a case they are forced to deal with intercession by interested parties. Since these cases often involve friends, relatives, leading cadres and other bigwigs, those handling cases fear unnecessary trouble. Also, some unit leaders find it a personal affront when public security organs catch their own men. Thus shamed, they do all they can to win face back, including exerting tremendous pressure.

2. Low-calibre cadre police soft on crime. A minority of cadre police, swayed by personal appeals or influenced by personal interests, find ways to exonerate criminals. Even when the facts are clear and evidence is conclusive in the case they are handling, they abandon the case because the criminal and litigant withdraw their testimonies. Some alter the nature of cases, writing off crimes such as rape or robbery as common hooliganism. Some officers undervalue the worth of stolen goods so that the criminals are not dealt with as severely as they should be. Other

officers are simply unprofessional and shy away from detailed on-the-scene investigations. Thanks to their laziness, a lot of evidence that should have been gathered is left untouched, and criminals that should fall into their hands get away scot-free.

3. Authorities put themselves above the law, mete out fines in place of sentences. Over the course of handling cases, some unit leaders with hazy conceptions of the law put themselves above the law and let their personal authority speak for the law. This way, cases in which an arrest should be made or a guilty party sent for labour education are handled in other ways. Some, thinking that money is everything, impose fines instead of sentences. When fines are paid, all is forgiven.

Public Security Squeezed, Criminals Sit Pretty

1. Public security budgets tight, manpower short. A common problem among public security organs today is serious under-funding; there may not always be enough money to handle cases, and manpower is insufficient. Consequently, efficiency drops and opportunities are missed, while criminals end up sitting pretty.
2. Backwards investigative techniques: These days criminals are getting sneakier about committing crimes and increasingly ingenious in their methods. They band into crime groups, hit on the run, and make use of vast areas in which to commit their treachery. Up against such competition, our crime-busting techniques are too feeble for the struggle. Also, we are poorly informed, making it impossible to solve a number of crimes swiftly, and weakening our effectiveness in fighting back against crime.
3. Shallow implementation of controls prevents a firm grip on social order. Some unit leaders are afraid that under the responsibility system they will come under fire from superiors when crimes are committed. As a result, they simply fail to report cases. Also, some members of the populace are so terrified of criminals that they shrink in the face of crime. Then there are others whose concepts of the law are weak, who know about cases but fail to report them,

or who even protect and assist criminals. Their interference makes it even tougher to catch criminals and solve cases, and criminals are not dealt the blows they should be.

Reward Honesty, Boost Pay

This writer suggests that public security organs adopt the following concrete measures to rectify their current ineffectiveness against crime:

1. Strengthen Party leadership over public security work so that public security work is put under the absolute leadership of the Party. Eliminate the privileged mindset of the very small minority of police cadres and establish whole-hearted dedication to serving the people. Establish close ties between the police and citizens, build the public security ranks into a potent force which can be completely trusted by the Party and the people.
2. Include public security work in the competition mechanism to reward excellence and discourage incompetence. Clearly define punishments and rewards; eliminate those who cannot adjust to public security work from the public security ranks. Offer higher pay to public security officers on the frontline so they need not to worry about making ends meet.
3. Fortify law enforcement mechanisms within public security organs. Supervisory mechanisms within public security, organs allow self-regulation, direction, and restraint, in-law enforcement activities. These are key elements enabling public, security organs to improve law enforcement activities, raise law enforcement levels, and ensure that they carry out their duties as prescribed by the law. In addition, various strict procedural systems, case evaluation systems, and case review systems can prevent a minority of cadre police from illegal handling of cases, allowing personal connections to interfere with cases, and. putting their own interests above the law to give criminals a free ride.
4. Initiate civil education, heighten, legal, consciousness. Carry out regular legal propaganda and education among all cadre police

and the broad masses to heighten legal concepts. This is not only meant to prevent public security, workers from trampling on the law because they allow personal interests to interfere but also to give the masses a clear understanding of the damage crime visits on society so as to prompt them to take up the struggle against various criminal activities.

5. Ensure appropriate crime-fighting budgets and improve equipment and facilities so that public security organs are fully equipped to take on crime and handle criminal cases with greater effectiveness. Government organs at all levels should include public security law enforcement expenses in their respective budgets and see that all expenses are faithfully reported.

ANNEX B

Transformation of Operational Mechanism of Industrial Enterprises[‡]

Since the promulgation of the Regulations on the Transformation of the Operational Mechanism of State Industrial Enterprises as a new start, the Chinese government has been urging for concerted efforts to work well for the transformation through a wide compaign of publicity. Premier Li Peng even raised the efforts to a high angle as to realize the important call of Deng Xiaoping to bring the national economy to a new stage during his trip to the south.

To revitalise the enterprises has always been a hard target of the country in its economic reform eversince the reform was put on the table. But it was only to be found later that as long as the operational mechanism of the enterprises was kept intact, it was very hard to keep their vigour stay. So it was fairly clear to many that whether the reform can go further to a deeper layer is wholly dependent on whether an adequate operational mechanism of the enterprises can be achieved. But to reach such a conclusion was surely not without a cost.

In the early stage of the reform and even one or two years ago, there was the unanimous reluctance to shift the traditional direct control of the government on the production and development of the enterprises. It was not until the operational vigour of most of the enterprises, especially that of part of the large- and medium-sized enterprises, had become so weak as to threaten their survival that

---

[‡]*Source*: This article appeared in *China Economic News*, 7 September 1992. It summarises the contents of three articles which appeared in *Jingji Ribao* 3, 4 and 7 September 1992 entitled respectively: "吹响企业走向市场的号角", "换换脑筋看条例" and "重点是落实企业自主权".

decisions were eventually made to push the enterprises into the market to fight for their own survival, and, correspondingly, to transform the operational mechanism of enterprises.

Success of the transformation depends on the government. In China, there are two stumbling blocks lying in the way to hinder the enterprises to go directly to the market: one, the government does not want to give the signal of going ahead; and the other, the enterprises do not want to do so by themselves.

More specifically, for such enterprises that are working under good efficiencies, the government does not want to let them go, but for those that are with poor efficiencies, the government cannot afford to let them go.

For a long time, the government had to make up for all losses suffered by the enterprises, who worked in red to keep them reproduced from other financial income. So now the turning of the mechanism is all up to the government. Only if the government gives the green light, the enterprises will have no reason not to face the market. But if the government is ready only to let the low-efficient ones go, transformation can hardly be successful.

It is to the comfort of the enterprises that the government has already made it straight that the transformation of the operational mechanism of enterprises depends for the first part on the transformation of the government function, without which, the former could not be achieved as expected. Furthermore, the transformation of the government function should be integrated with structural reforms of government offices.

Economists hold that for the latter reform, the central government should be put at the forefront and for that, a big change cannot be put forth until the meeting of the National People's Congress next year. Therefore, the work for the transformation in the enterprises is likely to remain in the stage of publicity and deliberation before that time.

Enterprises have already been given the right to make their own decisions since the promulgation of the "Law of Enterprises" four years ago. But due to all sorts of reasons, the law has not been carried out in full effect. The true implementation of the new regulations on the transformation of mechanism is a matter of popular concern. Now the determination and confidence of the government represented in its current relevant remarks are quite convincing. Presently economists based their optimism about the prospects on two facts: one, people are freeing their minds and changing their concepts following Deng Xiaoping's trip to the south to wipe out unfavourable factors; two, the new regulations are concrete in content, which are practicable and would not just be a scrap of paper.

ANNEX C

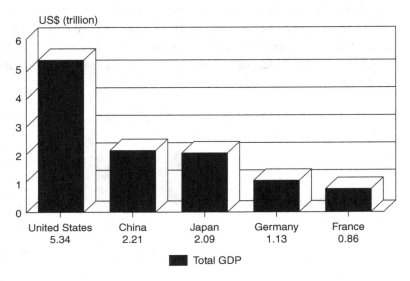

Total GDP.

Note: Converted to dollars using purchasing power adjusted exchange rates.

Source: "The Economics of the 1990s: Back to the Future" by Professor Lawrence H. Summers, in *The International Economy*, July/August 1992.

ANNEX D

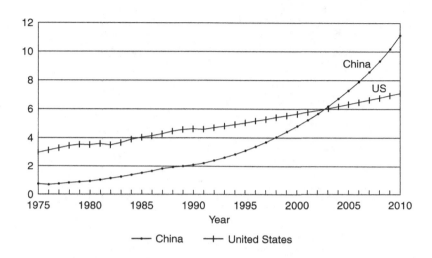

Total GDP at 1985 International Prices

If present trends were to contine, China will overtake the US as the world's largest economy by 2003.

Source: "The Economics of the 1990s: Back to the Future" by Professor Lawrence H. Summers, in *The International Economy*, July/August 1992.

9

China's Coal Industry: Symptom of a Deeper Malaise of the Economy*

Editors' Note

Coal has remained the major source of China's primary energy supply, meeting over 70% of China's primary consumption needs. In 1990, China produced just a little over one billion tons of coal; but today, the figure is 3.5 billion tons, in addition to a large amount of imports. China is always troubled by two basic problems from its coal industry. First, the coal output is far away from the populous South and East China, thereby presenting serious transportation and distribution problems. Second, China's coal industry was (is still today) plagued by a technological dualism: the better equipped and more advanced state-owned large coal miners vs. numerous small producers.

Goh Keng Swee and John Wong, in this joint report, discussed not just the growth and performance of China's coal industry in the early 1990s, but also its many structural problems arising from strict state planning control over the coal output and the pricing of coal. Much like other "strategic commodities", coal from state mines was sold at below cost, causing all state mines to suffer losses. But all state mines were SOEs operating on a soft budget constraint. The subsidised coal price might fit well with China's half-reformed economy then, but this distorted the market system of efficient allocation of resources while promoting wasteful consumption. What had most intrigued Goh and Wong was that the coal industry was then behaving much like a typical SOE at that time, with all its familiar malaise.

---

*Published by IEAP as *IEAP Discussion Paper No. 3* on 14 May 1991.

1. Introduction

China has the world's largest coal industry, which in 1990 produced over one billion tons of coal, from a mere 32 million tons in 1949. Today coal remains the cornerstone of China's energy sector, supplying 73% of China's primary energy consumption needs.

However, China's coal industry continues to be saddled with serious structural problems associated with production, consumption and investment. At one point, for instance, while coal was piling up around the mines in Shanxi province, Shanghai's power stations were reported to have only two days of coal reserves.

China has one of the world's largest proven coal reserves — in one estimate, as high as it would take 2,000 years to exhaust them at the current level of production. Since 80% of the economically recoverable reserves are away from the populous South and East, this aggravates the problem of coal transportation. The problem is further compounded by the fact that coal is a bulky commodity with high transportation cost while the transportation network itself happens to be the weakest link of the Chinese economy.

When the Communists took power in 1949, the large old mines formerly controlled by foreigners were nationalised and reorganised into the framework of central planning. Coal production increased sharply in the 1950s and, after the stagnation in the 1960s, picked up again in the 1970s. The 1980s saw another production upsurge.

The Chinese government has indeed made an effort to speed up the technological upgrading of the state mines and to improve their safety standards — hence the resultant growth in coal output. But it has singularly failed to introduce appropriate price reform to address the critical problem of efficiency. Thus the coal industry, which today boasts over 9,000 mines with nearly six million workers, operates at the level of productivity substantially below the national average, with 21% of mines making a loss.

Furthermore, the coal industry is loosely integrated, and it is plagued by technological or organisational dualism. Numerous small township and village mines (which are technically backward and unsafe) continue to exist along with the large state mines and the medium sized mines belonging to the provincial authorities.

This technological and organisational dualism produced an unexpected outcome to the coal industry's response to rapid increases in demand. The most backward sector, the ill-equipped small mines, supplied the largest share of increased supply between 1980 and 1988. Output nearly trebled and provided 190 million tons of the total increase of 360 million tons achieved during this period. The better equipped state and provincial mines supplied 89 million tons and 80 million tons respectively of the increase.

The reason for this lop-sided response is not difficult to find. Coal from state mines as well as coal from provincial mines handed over to the state were sold at below cost price in 1988, possibly even earlier. The 500 state mines suffered a loss of RMB 7.5 billion in 1990. Small mines sold their output in the free market. However, the free market operated mainly through government and private brokers without a properly organised wholesale market. Hence, inadequacy of information flows encouraged various kinds of abuses.

Raising the price of coal to more realistic levels will help the state and provincial mines. But without a marked improvement in rail and water transportation, industrial consumers will still face supply difficulties. But raising coal prices will transfer problems from state mines to the thousands of industrial consumers as the applications for price increases of their products will not be favourably considered in most cases. On the other hand, a general price increase of all "strategic" products and services such as energy, raw materials, semi-finished goods, transportation services will remove much of the waste caused by price distortions. But it will trigger off a huge cost-push inflation. This is something Beijing leaders dread.

In November 1989, the Central Committee of the Chinese Communist Party decided to re-centralise control over coal. All coal moving across provincial borders would be centrally managed by the State. The free market was to be eliminated and the two-tier price system gradually abolished. This recommendation provides the latest example of China's policy swings between liberalisation and centralisation.

2. Coal as a Vital Commodity

From a mere output of 32 million tons in 1949, China's coal output in 1990 had risen to just over one billion tons, making it the world's largest coal producer. Despite this impressive growth performance in aggregate terms, coal is one of the big basic industries in China today which continues to be saddled with serious problems in production, distribution and investment. Some of the problems are "structural" in nature, specific to the industry itself; others are born out of the general malaise of the total economic system. In short, the problems of the coal industry form the mirror image of the larger problems of China's heavy industry sector which need to be urgently addressed by the existing Chinese leadership in Beijing, be it "conservative" or "reformist".

The coal industry seems to be full of exasperating paradoxes which simply confound an outside observer. In 1989, when coal output breached the mark of one billion tons, there were reports of widespread shortages. While coal was piling up in mountains around the mines in Shanxi province, Shanghai's power stations at one point only had two days' reserves of coal. There are many large state mines which are mechanized (61% partly and 33% fully), selling their coal at RMB 35 per ton; but numerous small mines using primitive techniques have continued to survive, with some selling their coal for as high as RMB 300 per ton. Between 1985 and 1988 the sale price of coal for state mines increased from RMB 31.36 to RMB 36.43 per ton while their production costs shot up from RMB 29.33 to RMB 39.97 per ton.[1] Above all, China is notoriously inefficient in its consumption of energy; yet coal prices to urban consumers are set so low, only at a fraction of the international prices, that it

---

[1] J.P. Huang, "Fueling the Economy: China's Coal Producers can't Keep Up With Soaring Demand", *The China Business Review* (March–April 1991), p. 26.

certainly does not encourage conservation or help in reducing consumption demand.[2]

A unique feature of China's energy consumption is the high proportion of coal in both commercial and total energy consumption. In the early 1950s, coal constituted over 90% of China's total energy consumption. Today, notwithstanding the rapid growth of the petroleum industry, coal remains the cornerstone of China's energy sector, supplying 73% of China's primary energy consumption needs. The past decade has witnessed impressive progress in China's economic reform and open-door policy, especially in regard to a wide range of China's consumer goods industries. But the Chinese government did not seem to devote much of its reform efforts to tackling many inherent problems in an industry so basic and so vital as the coal industry.

It is not that China's top policy makers are unaware of the various problems in the coal industry. Gleaning through some of the important policy documents by the State Council on the coal industry, one cannot fail to be impressed that the Chinese government is genuinely concerned with the problems of the industry, such as technological upgrading of its many state-run mines and raising the safety standards in their operation.[3] In fact, the coal industry has achieved significant progress in the area of technological development with imported equipment, especially in

---

[2] China's inefficient use of energy is shocking. In 1980, according to a World Bank report, China's consumption of both commercial and total primary energy per unit of GDP was well above that of any major developed countries, doubling that of the US level and four times higher than Germany, France and Japan (*China: The Energy Sector*, Washington, DC, 1985, p. 11). In 1988 China's per capita energy consumption, at 580 kg of oil equivalent, was the second highest among the low-income countries, only next to oil producing Yemen (*World Development Report 1990*, p. 186). Clearly, China's existing economic system does not help energy saving.

[3] The development of the coal industry in the first three decades after the Communist rule and the broad reform plans for the 1980s are summarized in the volume, *China Coal Industry Yearbook 1983*. Compiled by the Ministry of Coal Industry, PRC and published by the Economic Information & Agency, Hong Kong (Hong Kong, 1984).

the 1980s. But the prices of most coal products have continued to be administered by government — at least for 75% of the nation's total coal output that goes through the state distribution network.

Why has the Chinese government all through these years not moved to rationalise the coal prices? Technological progress can of course increase efficiency, but this is expensive, requiring a lot of capital investment and training. However, a "good" policy change can also bring about greater efficiency. If the price distortion could be eliminated, i.e. coal prices be raised to more realistic levels, a great deal of problems inherent in the coal industry with regard to production, consumption and investment would be solved or at least alleviated. China's success in rural reform and the subsequent booming of many light industries as a result of price liberalisation clearly show that policy changes could be manipulated to realise many crucial economic goals.

Why has economic reform persistently eluded this old but vital industry? We cannot assume that the usually intelligent Chinese political leadership or at least its technical and professional staff do not understand this issue. The fact that it has not been effectively dealt with points to the extreme complexity of the problem as well as to the existence of numerous institutional constraints. The upshot nonetheless serves to show that China's economic reform of the past 10 years, successful as it is, has only scratched the surface of the economy, with many core areas still crying out for more determined reform efforts.

3. The Coal Industry: Growth and Structural Change

China already began to use coal for industrial and household purposes in the early centuries AD. When Marco Polo came to China in the 13th century, he saw that coal was "burnt throughout the province of Cathay".[4] Before the war coal had developed to be one of the few very large industries in China, even though most of the output came

---

[4] Tim Wright, *Coal Mining in China's Economy and Society, 1895–1937* (Cambridge, Cambridge University Press, 1984), p. 8.

from the large mines controlled by foreign interests, principally the British (in Kailuan) and the Japanese (in Fushun).

After the Communists came to power in 1949, the Ministry of Fuel was set up, with the responsibility of restoring production as well as transforming the "colonial" pattern of production organisation into one suitable for socialist planning. The coal industry, like such large smoke-stack industries as iron and steel, initially fitted in quite well the Stalinist type of central planning. Thus coal output doubled in the period of rehabilitation 1949–52, and it doubled again during the First Five-Year Plan period 1953–57. Then the irrational Great Leap Forward, 1958–59, led to another doubling of output, though much of which was of poor quality. Orderly development was resumed only in 1970. In 1979, at the start of economic reform, China produced 635 million tons of coal (Chart 1).

Production increases in the 1980s were quite impressive as they started off from a higher base. During 1980–88, coal output increased at the average rate of 5.8%, but still below the average GNP growth of 9.0% for the same period. By 1990 China's raw coal production increased to 1.08 billion tons (or 833 million tons of standard coal equivalent), with 45% of which being from the large mines under the state plan and with the remaining 55% from the provincial or local mines (Table 1). Ten years ago the distribution ratio was exactly the reverse, indicating that the smaller local mines had expanded their production more rapidly under decentralisation in the 1980s. The official output target for 2000 has been set for 1.4 billion tons.

In the 1950s, over 90% of China's total energy consumption came from coal. In 1989 coal still constituted 76% of total energy consumption, as opposed to 17% from oil, 2% from gas, and 5% from hydroelectricity (Chart 2 shows the relative shares of coal and oil in China's total energy production). Such heavy dependence on coal is primarily due to the existence of large, low-cost coal deposits (mainly bituminous), which can be found, in varying quantities, in almost every region of China. Proven reserves now stand at 900 billion tons, slightly behind those of the Soviet Union and the United States.

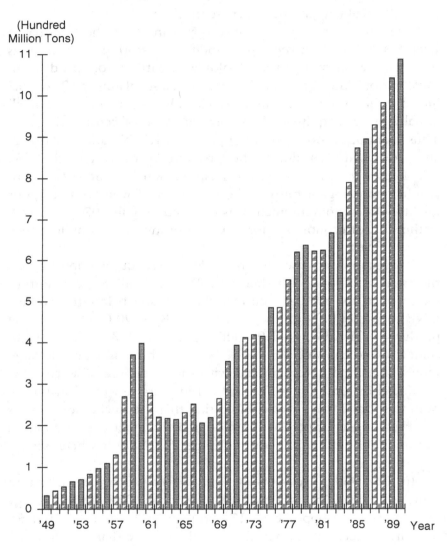

Chart 1: Total Production of Coal (1949–1990)

Source: State Statistical Bureau, *Zhongguo Nengyuan Tongji Nianjian 1989* (*China Energy Statistical Yearbook 1989*), Beijing, 1990. For 1989 and 1990 figures, *Renmin Ribao* (*People's Daily*, 12 April 1991).

Table 1. Coal Production in China

Year	Million tons	Composition (%)		
		State-owned mines	Local mines	Township and village mines
1949	32	75	25.00	
1950	43	69.77	30.23	
1951	53	69.81	30.19	
1952	66	72.73	27.27	
1953	70	74.29	25.71	
1954	84	73.81	26.19	
1955	98	74.49	25.51	
1956	110	74.55	25.45	
1957	131	71.76	28.24	
1958	270	58.52	41.48	12.59
1959	369	58.54	41.46	7.59
1960	397	60.45	39.55	5.54
1961	278	63.31	36.69	
1962	220	67.27	32.73	
1963	217	69.59	30.41	
1964	215	70.23	29.77	
1965	232	70.69	29.31	
1966	252	71.83	28.17	
1967	206	66.02	33.98	3.88
1968	220	66.82	33.18	5.91
1969	266	67.29	32.71	6.77
1970	354	64.12	35.88	8.76
1971	392	63.01	36.99	8.16
1972	410	60.73	39.27	8.78
1973	417	59.47	40.53	10.07
1974	413	58.84	41.16	12.59
1975	482	58.09	41.91	11.83
1976	483	56.73	43.27	13.46

(*Continued*)

Table 1. (*Continued*)

Year	Million tons	State-owned mines	Local mines	Township and village mines
			Composition (%)	
1977	550	53.64	46.36	14.36
1978	618	55.34	44.66	14.08
1979	635	56.38	43.62	15.43
1980	620	55.48	44.52	16.94
1981	622	53.86	46.14	18.81
1982	666	52.55	47.45	20.57
1983	715	50.77	49.23	22.24
1984	789	50.06	49.94	24.71
1985	872	46.56	53.44	27.29
1986	894	46.31	53.69	27.18
1987	928	45.26	54.74	28.12
1988	980	44.29	55.71	30.10
1989	1040			
1990	1085			

Source: State Statistical Bureau, *Zhongguo Nengyuan Tongji Nianjian 1989* (*China Energy Statistical Yearbook 1989*), Beijing 1990. For 1989 and 1990 figures, *Remin Ribao* (*People's Daily*), 12 April 1991.

But China's estimated reserves are as high as two trillion tons, or to take 2,000 years of exploitation at current levels of production to exhaust them.

However, the economically recoverable reserves are unevenly distributed, with 80% concentrated in North and Northeast China (40% in Shanxi alone), with the populous South and East being poorly endowed. This brings to the fore the complicated issue of coal transportation, with transportation itself being another weak link in the Chinese economy. The transportation bottleneck was by far the worst in Shanxi, which in 1984 had to ship its 120 million tons of coal

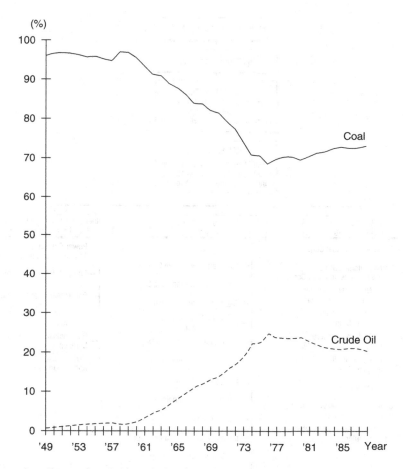

Chart 2: Shares for Coal and Crude Oil in China's Total Energy Production (1949–1988)

Source: State Statistical Bureau, *Zhongguo Nengyuan Tongji Nianjian 1989 (China Energy Statistical Yearbook 1989*, Beijing), 1990.

to 26 provinces throughout China and to export to 20 countries, thus heavily burdening its 3,000 km of railways.[5] Coal as a bulky commodity has high transportation costs, varying according to

---

[5] Vaclav Smil, *Energy in China's Modernization: Advances and Limitations* (Armonk, New York, M.E. Sharpe, 1988), p. 90.

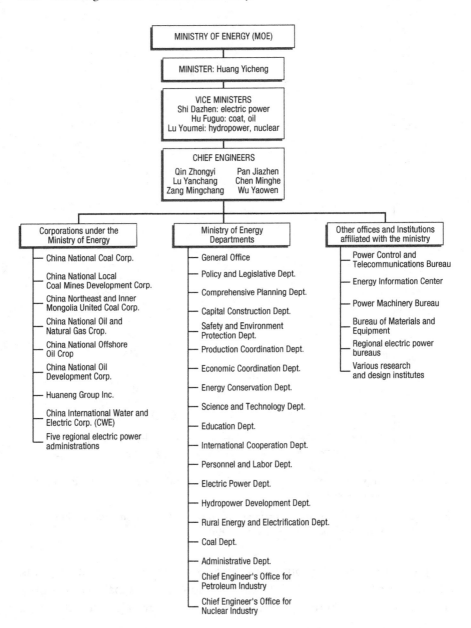

Chart 3: Organization Chart of the Ministry of Energy

Source: J. P. Huang, "Fueling the Economy: China's Coal Producers can't Keep Up With Soaring Demand", *The China Business Review*, March–April 1991, p. 25.

distance as well as the mode of transportation.[6] Thus, for years Chinese planners have been debating whether it should transport coal or transport electricity by first converting coal into electricity near the mines. Suffice it to say that the transportation bottleneck has much compounded the problems faced by the coal industry.[7]

In 1988 China's coal industry comprised 9,230 mines and employed a total of 5.6 million workers. 1,954 of these mines or 21% were reported to have made a loss totalling RMB3 billion. The industry's overall "efficiency" was well below the national average, with annual per-worker value added (productivity) only at RMB2,352 or just about 40% of the national level.[8] In 1990 China National Coal Development Corporation alone, which administers the 500 or so centrally-owned state mines, lost RMB7.5 billion, which had to be subsidized by the State. In the meanwhile, the state investment in the industry has not increased. During the Seventh Five-Year Plan, the government actually invested only RMB30 billion, falling short of the planned

---

[6] In China, before the war, land transportation costs for coal ranged upwards from around six cents per ton-km by cart, 10 cents by wheelbarrow, and 15–20 cents by pack animal, whilst only 0.2 cent by junk (Tim Wright, *op. cit.*, pp. 43–4). In early 1984, the average ex-mine price was about RMB 22 per ton. Railway was the dominant transportation mode, and typically consumers paid RMB 10 per ton or 45% of the ex-mine price, but this could be higher than RMB 30 per ton if road transportation was used. (The World Bank, *China: The Energy Sector*, 1985, p.77).

[7] Most of China's railways remain single track and unelectrified. In 1988 the volume of coal transported by railway increased by only 3.9% while coal production increased by 5.6% for that year. (J.P. Huang, *op. cit.*). The new double-track, electrified railway between datong and Qinhuangdao when in operation is expected to carry 100 million tons a year.

[8] State Statistical Bureau, *Zhongguo Gongye Jingji Tongji Nianjian 1989* (*China Industrial Economic Yearbook 1989*), Beijing, 1990. It should be noted that strictly speaking, the Chinese concept of efficiency in terms of value-added per worker is different from the conventional concept as applied to a market economy. In China, under state control the prices of many goods do not approximate marginal cost and hence the true level of efficiency cannot be reflected in the value-added concept. In the case of coal, part of the reason for the industry's relatively low value-added per worker is simply due to the fact that coal prices are set too low by the government.

RMB32 billion.[9] The coal industry thus seems to look like a declining industry.

Technological or organisational dualism is another structural problem of China's coal industry. Mining is organised at three levels. At the top are the 500 large mines directly controlled by the central government, which produce about 40% of total output. Then there are more than 1,600 medium-sized mines belonging to the provincial governments. Finally come the numerous small township and village mines, including many small open pits owned privately by peasants. As to be expected, a substantial gap exists between large mines and small mines in respect of technological development and productivity. In particular, many small mines are technically backward, inefficient, and unsafe; but ironically they owe their continuing existence to the high transportation costs associated with the coal produced from the large state mines. In the past, such dualism was deliberately promoted under Mao's "walking on two legs" development strategy, but it is now considered unviable under the new economic assumption.[10] In short, the coal industry as a whole needs to be better integrated.

4. The Need for Reform

An examination of Table 1 reveals some surprising facts about China's coal industry. The state-owned mines which received the best equipment paid for out of state funds contributed the least to the expansion of output. In 1980, output was about 345 million tons and by 1988 this increased to 434 million tons, a 26% increase. By contrast, township and village mines worked with primitive tools,

---

[9] J.P. Huang, *op. cit.* It is rather incomprehensive that the Chinese government has allowed the relative share of fixed investment for coal in the total energy sector to decline from 29.3% in 1984 to 16.4% in 1988, while the share for power generation has increased from 31.9% to 43.8% in the same period, since almost 80% of the power generation capacity is coal-fired [State Statistical Bureau, *Zhongguo Nengyuan Tongjii Nianjian 1989 (China Energy Statistical Yearbook 1989)*, Beijing, 1990].

[10] For a more detailed discussion of the small rural energy projects, see Robert P. Taylor, *Rural Energy Development in China* (Resource for the Future, Washington, DC, 1981).

picks and baskets usually. In 1980, their output was 105 million tons and by 1988, it had nearly trebled to 295 million tons. Provincial mines stood in between state and village mines, both in terms of technology and growth rates.

The question arises: "How did this happen? How did the tortoise outrun the hare?" It is tempting to seek answers in terms of stereotypes, e.g. the dead hand of bureaucracy stifling progress in state mines, or the lack of incentives to workers and management in state enterprises to perform better or even Janos Kornai's celebrated "soft-budget constraint". Each of these explanations contains an element of truth but none gets to the root of the matter. The root concerns prices and costs.

We noted in Section 2 that between 1985 and 1988, ex-mine prices of state coal increased from RMB 31.36 to RMB 36.43 per ton while costs increased from RMB 29.33 to RMB 39.97. By 1988, possibly even earlier, costs had exceeded prices. In Section 3, we noted that the 500 state mines lost RMB 7.5 billion in 1990. No information is available about the profitability of township and village mines, but we know that their output, at least up to 1989, did not enter the state plans and hence production and marketing were governed by market conditions. If they made profits, they produced; if they could not, they closed down.

We noted in Section 2 that the low prices set for State produced coal encouraged waste in consumption. Expanding output meant increasing producers' losses when prices were set below costs. Further the rapid economic growth generated by the reforms of the 1980s increased the demand for energy in all forms — electricity, oil and coal. The reforms decentralised production decisions of non-state enterprises. All these factors led to the emergence of a free market for coal not distributed through the state channels. Industrial consumers unable to get sufficient supplies through state channels were willing to pay RMB 300 or more per ton of coal. That was where township and village coal went and that was why output nearly trebled in eight years.

Some explanation of the coal distribution system will bring to light the tangled situation of the coal industry. Distribution has always been a messy business whether done through state channels or the free market. The matching of buyers and sellers of state produced coal takes place through an inter-agency conference with 600 participants lasting 100 days.[11] As for the free market, it does not function the way markets do in capitalist countries. There is no wholesale market or wholesale merchants carrying stocks. Not only is the transportation system overstretched but violent price fluctuations and the risk of sudden changes of government policy make stocking up too risky. The market consists of non-government brokers and representatives from various city and county "economic co-ordination offices". Because of inadequate information flows, malpractices of all kinds are liable to take place.[12] In spite of all these shortcomings, the free market serves the purpose of expanding coal production, though mostly from the most backward sector of the coal industry. This follows from the perverted relation of prices and costs in the advanced sector.

There is no quick fix to the difficulties of the coal industry. Raising coal prices to realistic levels is a necessary but not sufficient condition for a solution. It is also necessary to improve rail transportation as well as sea and river transportation, and all these will take time and money. The necessary funds will have to come from the state budget, already sorely pressed by competing needs. Transportation services, being graded essential, are offered at low prices so that they generally cannot generate sufficient profits to pay for development costs. [In Singapore, we make sure that the Public Utilities Board (PUB), Telecoms and the Port of Singapore Authority (PSA) turn out sufficient surpluses and hence are unfamiliar with the situation in China where the norm is for state enterprises to lose money.]

Leaving aside rail transportation, what stands in the way of raising prices of state-controlled coal output? There are both ideological and practical difficulties. Ideologically, "essential" or "strategic" products and services such as coal, petroleum, electricity, raw materials, semi-finished goods (steel products), railways, machine tools and machinery, represent the economic strength of the nation and must be supplied

---

[11] J.P. Huang, *op. cit.*, p. 26.
[12] Information from our own correspondent.

at the lowest possible price. Their production and distribution are determined by the State Planning Commission (SPC) which sets quotas for enterprises, approves prices and assigns output to eligible purchasing enterprises.

A product like coal has thousands of industrial consumers, e.g. power plants, steel mills, chemical plants and all industries using boilers for heat or energy. As many of these operate at the margin of profitability or, more likely, already incur losses, an increase in coal price will increase their losses proportionately as they normally will not be allowed to raise prices of their output. The routine procedures state enterprises have to follow in applying for price increases ensure that, in practice, these enterprises will not go through them as the easy option of getting more largesse from the state coffers is readily available. So what is saved in the state budget through smaller subsidies to state mines has to be spent on increased subsidies to industrial consumers of coal.

From this, it is clear that raising the price of one strategic product will not only be a messy exercise but also a pointless one. To have a beneficial effect, price reforms must be comprehensive and include all the essential goods and services whose prices had been kept well below what economists call the "equilibrium" level, that is the level at which long-term supply and demand will be brought into equality. Generally, such prices should approximate international prices of equivalent goods.

There is, however, a major obstacle to implement a solution of this kind. It will trigger off an enormous cost-push inflation. The reason is that most controlled prices were set at well below international levels. That is why Beijing leaders prefer the present state of affairs however unsatisfactory and wasteful it is. On 9 November 1989, the Party's Central Committee published a "Decision" on certain economic policies and directly referred to the problems of the coal industry.

According to this document, the State should control not only the output of state mines and coal handed over by provincial mines to the State, but also all coal transported beyond provincial boundaries for centralised distribution, ordering, transportation and management. Only state-approved agencies could participate in the coal business. The free market must be eliminated as it was designed "to seek huge profits, disrupt the market and boost prices". That the free market was the consequence of shortages caused by unrealistic price control was overlooked.

In 1990 and 1991, the "double-tier" prices of coal subject to central allocation would be phased out and replaced by a single price. After this, more goods would be brought under central allocation and the single price system.

The trouble with this approach is that it had been tried before and failed. There is no reason to expect a different outcome this time. Since 1979, China's economic policy has alternated between one extreme and the other. This disposition has been aptly condensed into the Chinese political *cheng-yu* or idiom: 一抓就死, 一放就乱. Freely translated in this context, it means, "Centralisation leads to stagnation, liberalisation leads to chaos."

10

Doing Business in China*

Editors' Note

This was the speech made by Goh Keng Swee at the gathering of foreign business people in Paris in 1994. China's economy was then booming with double-digit rates of growth. In fact, the economy was getting overheated because of the massive influx of foreign direct investment following Deng Xiaoping's Nanxun. Many foreign investors were bullish about investing in the newly opened-up China. As many of them were unfamiliar with China's institutional structure, they were also worried about the potential risk of doing business there.

Goh's basic message was that while he would continue to be optimistic about China's future growth potential, he also advised potential investors to be wary of problems arising from China's different business culture and different operating environment. Foreigners would have to get used to China's different legal system, banking and taxation systems and so on.

China is such a large country presently undergoing dramatic economic changes as she presses forward with economic reforms. Since the reforms began in 1979, literally thousands of pieces of legislation — principal and subsidiary — have been passed by the central government, provincial governments and local governments.

---

*Speech delivered to the Institute De L'Enterprise in Paris on 18 May 1994.

151

One Hong Kong legal firm engages nine lawyers on full-time work in tracking such legislation.

The difficulty one faces concerns the degree of detail and depth with which a subject should be treated.

First, China is a large country. Size in itself is not significant. In the case of China, large size has given rise to differences of perception. Jiangsu is so different from Xinjiang, and Henan from Guangdong. When we consider that nine provinces each has population larger than 50 million, that is, that they are as large or larger than any West European state, our minds begin to boggle at the implications.

The second reason is that reliable information is more difficult to get in China than in most other countries. This is especially worrying because their method of government and ways of doing business differ from what businessmen are accustomed to elsewhere.

Despite these troublesome problems, businessmen all over the world seem to be flocking to China in search of investment opportunities. These are incontrovertible facts. What is less certain is whether all this excitement and optimism rest on solid grounds.

At a time when advanced industrial countries without exception were gripped in the throes of a recession the last two years, China registered double-digit growth rates, 14% last year, and still going strong now. In fact, China's worry is not recession but overheating. The Chinese government is taking strong measures to reduce the growth rate while the industrial countries are striving to increase theirs. Any Western government that can achieve 3% growth rate this year for its economy would earn the gratitude of its citizens.

While the attractiveness in investing in China can be understood in general terms, the intending investor has special concerns. He either invests his own money or, if he is a corporate executive, the money of shareholders. In either case, large sums are involved and have to be committed over a period of years. This process inevitably involves risk as nobody, however well-informed, can foresee the future with certainty.

Investment risk in this sense can be conveniently discussed under two heads: "specific risk" and "general risk". By specific risk I mean the business risk arising from putting your money in a given location and a given line of business. This could be a hotel in Qingdao or a ball-point pen factory in Wuxi or whatever.

The general risk of investing in China is defined as follows. I assume that before you make your investment decisions, you have collected all the information needed to make rational calculations of rates of returns. This will include the working environment in your selected locality, the standing of the local enterprise if you decide on a joint-venture form of enterprise, market prospects, cost structure, laws and regulations relating to the industry, etc.

The general risk then relates to the future performance of China's economy. Can it continue with the robust rate of expansion, averaging 9% since 1979? Even if the answer to this question is "yes", what about this overheating business? Will the measures introduced by Vice Premier Zhu Rongji result in some kind of credit crunch? If so, why not wait?

I will first try to answer the question about long-term growth prospects before attending to China's current situation. I believe China's long-term prospects are good and if they continue with their economic reforms to increase the role of the free market to determine use of resources, their rate of expansion in the next 10 years should be as good as that of the last 10.

What are the reasons for this optimistic view? To put a complex subject in simple terms, one can say that the way China's economy is growing today resembles in some important respects, the way the economies of Taiwan and South Korea grew in the three post-war decades. These economies grew at double-digit rates for much of this period.

These economies began from a low base, that is, with low per capita national incomes and a large reserve of farm workers to provide workers when their manufacturing and service industries expanded. But where did the push into these new activities come from? The push came mainly from the acquisition of scientific and engineering knowledge. Koreans and Taiwanese first acquired this knowledge in American universities but they quickly expanded technical education in their own countries. Their achievements in this field have not been adequately recognised by growth economists who sought to explain their success mainly in terms of low-cost labour and high rates of savings and investment. These are the usual variables used by growth economists in explaining the economic miracles achieved by these two countries. They do perform a useful explanatory role but they do not reach the fundamentals.

Consider the progress of technical education in South Korea the last two decades. In 1991, their universities and polytechnics had 474,000 or 45% of total student enrolment, studying the hard sciences and their applications to production such as engineering, agriculture, fisheries, medicine and pharmacy. In engineering there was a heavy concentration on microelectronics.

In addition to home-trained technical personnel, South Korea had sent large numbers of students to the USA, many of whom have returned. The same situation exists in Taiwan. There was a huge brain drain in the 1950s and 1960s, but eventually a large number of these returned to Taiwan equipped not only with university education, but also with production and management experience in American corporations. 19,018 out of 112,659 of those who left had returned by 1988. Their efforts were supplemented by huge numbers of locally-trained graduates. Enrolment in Taiwan's 117 universities and polytechnics in the engineering faculty came to 173,000 in 1989. The number graduating each year, in relation to population, is 35% higher than that of the USA. University education in terms of student enrolment expanded 10 times in the last 40 years in these two countries.

In seeking an explanation for the spectacular performance of the domestic industries of these two countries in the world's export markets, we need to look no further than the combination of these trained scientific, engineering and technical personnel with the increasing workforce supplied by the rural population as farms shed surplus workers in the course of modernisation of agriculture. Even so, wages have increased substantially but this has not dampened export growth.

Much the same combination of knowledge and surplus labour exists in China. Between 1952 and this decade, the output of scientists and engineers in China increased by 20 times, twice the increase in Korea and Taiwan. Each year, some 200,000 engineers and 30,000 natural scientists graduate from China's 1,070 tertiary education institutions. The numbers may be small in relation to population and production requirements, but the aggregate effect in expanding production capacity is large. The impact on industrial output and economic growth was, however, limited and remained below those of Korea and Taiwan until the reforms were launched in 1979. Since then, as we know, China's growth rates have reached the same heights. But there are important differences in the way industrial output increased.

While in the two countries, a large part of industrial output was exported, in China the major part was directed to domestic use. Further, while output was produced by private enterprise in the two, in China, state-owned enterprises (SOEs) had a virtual monopoly of output under the centrally planned system in operation since 1949 for some 30 years. These differences in production system have had important consequences.

First, whereas products of the two have reached world standards in the export markets, China's products sold in the domestic market have not. Her exports consist mainly of labour-intensive, low-technology goods such as textiles, garments, toys and suchlike. Second, competition between export industries in Taiwan and Korea ensures the weeding out of enterprises handicapped by incompetent managements. This process is virtually unknown among SOEs. Those who lose money for whatever reason receive subsidies from the state budget. So the unfit continue to survive.

Third, while product improvement and cost reduction among export industries form a vital part of the business strategy of Taiwan and Korean enterprises, this is not widely practised among China's state enterprises. Improvements in production processes have usually been made to depend on imports of foreign technology, often involving the purchase of complete sets of plants with large expenditure of hard currency.

The post-1979 reforms have introduced, on an increasing scale, competition between SOEs, both in the sale of the output and in the purchase of raw materials and components. But competition in the factor markets — for labour, managerial personnel and funds — remains restricted. This regards increases in efficiency in many ways, principally by reducing incentives to excel.

One reason for the caution in liberalising factor markets is the leadership fear of its disruptive effects. SOEs employ large excesses in their workforce. Some estimates place this surplus workforce at 20 million. Unless alternative employment can be found for them or a social security system is in place to provide a safety net, China's leaders consider the gain in economic efficiency created by competition in the factor markets will be outweighed by social discontent caused by 20 million workers suddenly losing their jobs.

In assessing the long-term prospects of the Chinese economy, we note that economic forecasting is a dangerous undertaking. But I believe China can continue to grow at between 8% to 12% in most years over the next two decades, just as Korea and Taiwan did at a similar stage of their development.

The above projection rests on certain assumptions which should be spelt out. The first is that the reforms will continue — which should have no difficulty. The problem area centres on political reforms. Students of the Chinese economy increasingly detect trouble at the many points where the political and economic systems interface. Consider two examples. People in top management positions in both government and business are obviously underpaid in relation to their responsibilities. Rectifying this anomaly runs into political, not economic resistance. In Marxist ideology, the working class forms the most advanced class of society. Hence, it is not politically acceptable that business and government executives get salaries appropriate to their responsibilities, because these will be so much higher than what workers get.

Next, how do we explain the absence of a modern legal system in China in spite of efforts to introduce one? There are several reasons, but the major one arises from the political system, which rests on the supremacy of the Communist Party of China. An independent judiciary occupies a pivotal position in a modern legal system and no one has yet found a way of reconciling the conflicting claims of Party supremacy and judicial independence.

Political reform is an extremely complex subject on which little research has been done mainly because of the difficulty in getting reliable information. The subject comes under virtual taboo among intellectuals in China. Outside China, the issue becomes mainly one of the uniformed propaganda in the Western media. Nevertheless I believe that political reforms will, before many years, occupy an important place in the country's agenda.

The second assumption concerns education, particularly tertiary education. Success in economic reforms in China has had an unexpected impact on the institutions which provided the impulse for growth — the 1,070 universities and polytechnics which trained the brain power to master the material sciences. As salaries, wages, bonuses and incomes have generally increased in the enterprise sector, university employees still work on fixed salaries. As a result, they have to moonlight; some professors, it is reported, work as hawkers in their off-duty hours. Not unexpectedly, universities find it increasingly difficult to recruit talent. It is not difficult to set these matters right but the Chinese system of rigid control of pay scales based on egalitarian notions to which I have referred, can make adequate and timely adjustments more difficult than they would be in, say, Singapore.

The Chinese are aware of these difficulties and are addressing their minds to them. Before leaving the subject of market competition, I should mention the township and village enterprises (TVEs). These are a uniquely Chinese invention. They began to proliferate in 1984–85 and since then their outputs have registered scarcely credible rates of increases. Many of them regard 30% to 50% annual growth rates as commonplace. Needless to say, these operate in a completely competitive market for products, raw materials (in most cases), labour, funds, and, most important, management and know-how. A good part of the fast growth rates of the Chinese economy can be traced to the performance of TVEs.

If growth rates in China approximate those of Korea and Taiwan in the earlier decades, the Chinese economy will reach gigantic proportions within the lifetime of most of you gathered here. China is already the world's largest producer of coal and cement and the fourth largest producer of steel, producing more than 80 million tonnes a year. When it reaches a mature stage, steel production will exceed 500 million tonnes a year and a vehicle output of 50 million a year. She is likely to be the largest producer of almost any important commodity. But we can look at these figures from another angle. It shows that China has still a long way to go and will take many years to get there. And she will have to modify her economic, social and political institutions which she has inherited from the recent past and which has brought about so many problems.

That is the long-term future in the optimistic scenario. What about the present, especially the overheating of the economy? This represents one of the many problems I just mentioned. The present situation is not the result of human error or bad judgement on the part of the Finance Minister, the Central Banker, the State Planning Commission, the Prime Minister — whoever or whatever. It is the inevitable outcome, one is tempted to say, of the economic, social and political institutions through which central, provincial and local leaders make their decisions and carry them out.

Of course, industrial economies of the West also experience business cycles but their governments have learnt to moderate the intensity of fluctuations by fiscal and monetary policies. For this purpose, they use their central banks to influence money supply and use national taxes to influence aggregate demand. In China, these levers of macro control, as they are called, can be considered weak or non-existent. Hence, fluctuations in output and prices attain greater amplitude than in the capitalist West. Overheating occurs every four years or so, in 1980, 1984/85, 1988/89 and now in 1993/94.

For a somewhat simplified account of why and how business cycles occur in China, as with other countries, our enquiry begins with the banking system. China has a central bank, the People's Bank of China (PBOC), and several specialised banks such as the Agricultural Bank, Industrial and Commercial Bank of China, the Bank of China, the Construction Bank of China and so on. These specialised banks originally catered for defined sectors of the economy, as indicated by their names, but today some overlapping takes place in order to promote competition.

These specialised banks do not operate the same way as our commercial banks do. Our banks have complete autonomy on loan decisions. Neither the government nor the Monetary Authority of Singapore (MAS) can order any bank to lend money to a given customer or for a given project. In China, 80% of bank loans are determined by those in authority and, hence, these loans are called "policy loans". The natural result of this arrangement is that banks are not responsible for profits and losses. If a loan turns bad, the bank cannot be blamed. Banks in China function principally as the government's cashiers.

What about the Central Bank — the PBOC? It does not have independent powers to control money supply. It acts as the government's chief cashier, supplying funds to the specialised banks at the request of the authorities. It does not even have the power to set the interest rates at which these loans may be made. So, while central banks in advanced economies function as lenders of last resort, the PBOC's role is lender of first resort, in keeping with its role of chief cashier.

A banking system of this kind works well when the State Planning Commission in Beijing determines all the goods and services the country produces. It is a logical adjunct to the centrally planned command economy. But when production responds increasingly to market forces and less to planning decisions, trouble develops in a number of ways. The economic reforms have decentralised decisions on production. Much of the authority exercised by the Centre has devolved to the provinces, and from these to the cities and municipalities.

This devolution of authority happens not only with enterprises engaged in production but also within the entire banking system, including the PBOC. Provincial branches of the PBOC are manned by employees of the provincial governments though the appointment of the chairman must be agreed with Beijing. Much of the same arrangements apply to the specialised banks. Thus the entire banking system is vulnerable to political pressure from provincial and local governments to provide funds for projects and enterprises in their localities.

Consider the likely outcome of these arrangements between banks and state enterprises. In the 1980s, the ability to produce in terms of know-how and workforce expanded rapidly. At the same time there was a shortage of goods of all kinds. Once bank loans were made available to producers, output soon went on-stream, the economy was expanded, confidence was generated and the upswing of the business cycle began its leap forward. Eventually, the economy ran into supply bottlenecks and price increases provided clear evidence of overheating.

Banks in capitalist countries are constrained in their lending operations in two ways. First, the creditworthiness of the borrower must be addressed since bad loans damage their balance sheets. Second, total loans advanced must be kept within bounds in relation to the statutory reserve requirements. These constraints do not apply in China. Policy loans are a responsibility of the government. As for statutory reserves, the PBOC, as the chief cashier, usually keeps banks amply provided with funds, that is, until central government decides to rein in the volume of bank credit, as has happened now.

A major difficulty the Chinese government has to labour under is the absence of fiscal (or budgetary) levers. One way of cooling down an overheated economy is to increase tax rates. In China, the fiscal lever cannot easily be used. While Beijing lays down tax rates, collection is done by provincial and local governments. These take upon themselves a wide area of discretion. Further, the division of tax proceeds between Centre and provinces is carried out under a complex system of negotiations. In 1978, before the reforms began, state revenue amounted to 31.2% of GNP. By 1991, this had been reduced to 18.2%. The result has been that control over the economy rests almost solely on monetary policy.

Since the banking system provides no leverage to the Central Bank to control money supply through interest rates or open market operations, the central government must rely on administrative measures. That happened in 1989 and is being repeated today. But there is an important difference between Premier Li Peng's 1989–91 credits crunch and Vice Premier Zhu Rongji's more moderate and more discriminating approach.

One result of the 1989–91 credit crunch was the huge rise of a chain of debts among SOEs. 'When short of funds, an SOE would not pay its bills for materials supplied by other SOEs. When all SOEs behaved in this way, the knock-on effects could be serious. Last year, Vice Premier Zhu was assigned the task of solving this debt-chain problem which he did with efficiency and despatch. This explains why he has avoided applying emergency brakes to the economy as Premier Li Peng did.

Vice Premier Zhu aims to bring off a soft landing for the economy. If he can engineer a soft landing, it will be a spectacular achievement, but whether the landing is soft or hard, he will succeed in moderating inflationary pressures and getting a better balance between money supply and production in important sectors of the economy.

Economists accustomed to conventional wisdom about economic growth will feel uneasy over use of bank credit creation by the Central Bank as a means of financing increases in investment. Neo-classical economic theory asserts that such investment must be financed out of real savings. This was not the way China expanded production. Was it wrong or unsound?

The best response is not to argue about theory but to look for similarities in the experience of other countries. We find that Japan in the first two and a half decades of her economic miracle financed her industrial expansion in much the same way as China is doing today, that is, extending Central Bank loans to commercial banks. But the Japanese took stringent measures to control inflationary pressures that must build up on two fronts — the balance of trade and domestic prices. The trade balance was kept on an even keel through import and foreign exchange controls and the encouragement to export. Domestic prices were subject to price control, reinforced by fiscal policy. The key measure was the avoidance of budget deficits. Central bank money was never used to finance government expenditure.

It is in this last item that China's experience differs from Japan's. Because of the weakness of the tax collection machinery and the large subsidies paid to loss-making SOEs, deficits have remained high and resort to Central Bank credit unavoidable. The worse effects of inflationary pressure have been dampened by the ability of China's economy to expand production. This ability, as I explained, rests on the growing number of scientists and engineers combined with a large reserve of rural labour force.

In a strange way, China's experience seems to support one of Lord Keynes's central theories, now all but forgotten. This states that when there are unemployed resources available in any economy, a government can finance expansion by bank credit expansion without fearing runaway inflation. But the experience of Japan and China shows that while you can do this for a while, you must take countermeasures in time.

Vice Premier Zhu Rongji's countermeasures will work, perhaps with less disruption than that which accompanied Premier Li Peng's policies in 1989–91. We do not have sufficient information to say when normal growth will be restored, but it will be. In effect, what I am saying is that China's long-term growth prospects are good and the risk of investing in China belongs to the category I called "specific risk".

This requires the intending investor to do his homework diligently, that is to say, to collect reliable information in China relevant to his project. I hope you will not consider I am taking undue advantage of your hospitality in telling you that I am Chairman of two institutions in Singapore concerned with getting information about the Chinese economy — the Institute of East Asia Political Economy and the East Asian Consultancy. The first is an academic research institute staffed mainly by researchers who started their career in China and migrated to America or Europe, from where we recruited them. The second offers Singapore investors assistance in the early stages of their attempts to invest in China in collecting information, identifying possible joint-venture partners and helping in getting negotiations started. We shall be glad to offer you the same services.

II

The Awakening of Asia's
Giant — China*

Editors' Note

From the start of economic reform in 1979 to 1994, China's economy was growing at nine per cent. Asia's giant had awakened, with its 1.2 billion customers beckoning. Goh Keng Swee explained this phenomenon as a competent economist himself to the many professional securities analysts in Singapore. He reminded the audience that China's rapid economic growth did not start from Deng Xiaoping's reform in 1979. China had laid down a good industrial foundation in its First Five-Year Plan (1952 to 1957). Goh was always impressed by China's high education policy which put heavy emphasis on science and engineering (over 60% of undergraduate students). This along with the market reform had contributed to China's high economic growth.

At the same time, Goh also cautioned that China was still facing the problem of how to complete its unfinished business of reform. Until then, China's economy would continue to face many problems of the half-reformed economy associated with inherent macroeconomic instability (the boom-bust cycles), the inefficiencies of the SOEs and the complicated central-local relationship for a country with five levels of government. Singaporeans living in a small island state with no local government would certainly be flabbergasted when Goh said the central government in Beijing would have to deal with "more than 50,000 (local) governments"!

---

*Speech delivered at the 16th Asian Securities Analyst Council Conference on 12 September 1994 at Westin Stamford Hotel, Singapore.

If asked to cite the year the Chinese giant woke up, most people would choose 1979 when Mr. Deng Xiaoping started the reforms of China's economy which produced such dramatic results. Annual economic growth since then averaged 9%. Today, it is hardly an exaggeration to say that businessmen in Western industrial countries are dazzled by the prospects offered by the huge burgeoning market of 1.2 billion customers.

But 1979 is the wrong answer. The giant woke up 30 years earlier (see Table 1). According to an IMF report of February 1981,[1] between 1949 and 1952, the national income grew at an average of 19.3%, gross industrial output at 34.8%. During the First Five-Year Plan, growth moderated somewhat, income grew at 8.9% a year, industrial output at 18.0%.

Let us find out what happened during the early years to explain such an unprecedented performance. Part of the reason can be traced to the unification of this huge country by the victory of the Communist Party of China, ending a century of unending turmoil

Table 1.   Annual Average Growth Rates

	National income	Gross agricultural output	Gross industrial output
1949–52	19.3%	14.1%	34.8%
1953–57 First FYP	8.9%	4.5%	18.0%
1958–62 Second FYP	−3.1%	−4.3%	3.8%
1963–65 Recovery from Great Leap	14.5%	11.1%	17.8%
1966–70 Third FYP	8.4%	3.9%	11.7%
1971–75 Fourth FYP	5.6%	4.0%	9.1%
1976–79 Fifth FYP	6.2%	5.4%	9.3%

Source: IMF, *The People's Republic of China: Recent Economic Developments*, 13 February 1981, p 6.

---

[1] IMF — *The People's Republic of China: Recent Economic Developments*, 13 February 1981, Table 1 on p. 6.

which began with the First Opium War in 1840. Some may argue that beginning from a low base, it was not difficult to achieve high rates of growth, provided you had strong leadership. But this is only a partial explanation. Some economists argue that the poorer the country is, the more difficult it is to get rich.[2] Economic theory states that since the poor save less than the rich, poor countries cannot save enough to provide for large investments needed to push the economy forward.

The major push to the economy in the early years came from the large economic aid supplied by the former Soviet Union to start China's industrialisation programme.[3] Not only were both countries of immense size but they both ran what we now call centrally planned economic systems, or command economies. Central planners of giant economies share another common trait. They give high priority to heavy industry. Thus, the Soviet Union aided projects between 1949 and 1959 set up 156 large industrial enterprises; of these 21 were in iron and steel and non-ferrous metals; 27 in electric power stations, and no less than 63 in the machine building industries.

Soviet aid took several forms:

(i) building of complete plants;
(ii) providing equipment and machinery;
(iii) stationing of experts to help China build and operate these plants — some 11,000 specialists went to China between 1950 and 1960;
(iv) supplying technical specifications and designs for construction — more than 10,000 during this decade;
(v) training of Chinese students, technicians and scientists in Russia — more than 36,000 took part.

[2] Lester Thurow, *Head to Head: The Coming Economic Battle Among Japan, Europe, and America*, New York: William Morrow &. Co., Inc., 1992.

[3] Cheng Chu-yuan, *Economic Relations Between Peking and Moscow: 1949–63*, New York: Frederick A. Praeger, 1964. See also Li Choh-ming, "China's Industrial Development, 1958–63", pp. 175–210; *China Under Mao: Politics Takes Command*, edited by Roderick MacFarquhar, Cambridge: The Massachusetts Institute of Technology Press, 1966.

Sino–Soviet co-operation was effective — as the IMF statistics showed. One party had the technology and the other party supplied competent and willing learners. The relation between teacher and pupil was doubtless made comfortable because both were fervent believers in Marxist socialist ideology. However, this socialist camaraderie ran into trouble in the late 1950s.

We need not concern ourselves about the rights and wrongs of the dispute between them, which became increasingly open and acrimonious. Let us look at the economic outcome. During China's Second Five Year Plan, 1958–62, her national income declined at an average of 3.1% a year. You will recall that this was the period when Chairman Mao was dissatisfied with growth rates of 19.3% and 8.9% recorded previously. He launched the Great Leap Forward. It turned out to be an unmitigated disaster. More damaging than the fall of national income was the decline in agricultural output averaging 4.3% over five years. When the population had just enough to eat to begin with, a decline of this magnitude must have inflicted enormous suffering.

Following the Second Five-Year Plan's ended in 1962, China put in two years' effort aimed at undoing the damage. The economy rebounded quickly, with national income growing at 14.5% a year and farm output at 11.1%. The Third Five-Year Plan, 1966–70, witnessed a revival of Chairman Mao's practice of permanent revolution. This time the effort was thoroughly orchestrated and reached new heights of recklessness, I refer, of course, to the Great Proletarian Cultural Revolution. Strangely, despite the upheavals caused by the Red Guards, the economy did not suffer. National income grew at 8.4% a year, agricultural output at 3.9%. The reasons for this outcome are unclear. Perhaps the Red Guards vented their rage on persons and cultural objects such as ancient temples. Or perhaps those in charge of economic affairs had learnt from previous experience how to work out methods of damage limitation.

During the two following Five-Year Plans, between 1971 and 1979, growth moderated to just under 6%, agriculture at 5.5%, industry at 9.2%. These growth rates would be judged satisfactory in developing countries and, in fact, exceeded the target set by the UN development experts — 5% GDP annual growth. But these figures concealed major flaws which the leaders under Mr. Deng Xiaoping saw through. There was an enormous waste of resources when state enterprises produced not what consumers wanted, but what central planners decided. The lack of competition encouraged inefficient production.

Before we discuss what these are, let me return to the subject of the build-up of technology which the Soviet Union introduced to China during 1949–59. This great effort set China briskly on the path of industrialisation but when it ended in 1962, China was able to make further advances on her own devices. To assess her progress in this field we must examine the expansion of her education system, shown in Table 2.

We note that the number of tertiary education Institutes more than trebled in 30 years, the increase in secondary schools was almost as big. We can now examine enrolment figures in Table 3.

These figures show an explosion in attendance at educational institutions. One important detail should be mentioned here — the

Table 2.   Education Statistics — Number of Institutions

	Number		
Year	1949	1965	1980
Tertiary Institutes	205	434	675
Secondary Schools	1,171	1,265	3,669
Primary Schools	356,769	1,681,939	917,316

Source: Educational Statistics Yearbook of China 1992.

Table 3.   Education Enrolment

	Number	
Year	1949	1980
Tertiary Institutes	117,129	1,175,304
Secondary Schools	1,270,050	57,478,300
Primary Schools	24,391,100	146,270,000

Source: Educational Statistics Yearbook of China 1992.

Table 4. Number Graduating in Various Disciplines, 1949–49

Engineering	1,073,000
Natural Sciences	223,500
Agriculture, Medicine, etc.	374,500
Teacher Training	636,600
Others (humanities, economics, etc.)	374,470
Total	2,682,070

Source: Educational Statistics Yearbook of China 1992.

number of graduate students enrolled in universities increased from a bare 629 in 1949 to 21,604 in 1980. It has since increased to 94,164 by 1992. How were students distributed among the faculties? We expect a concentration in engineering and science and this is what happened. The numbers graduating between 1949 and 1979 are given in Table 4.

Table 4 shows a heavy concentration on the natural sciences and their applications in engineering, agriculture, medicine, etc. These accounted for some 62% of the total and, doubtless, is the result of state policy of increasing the country's productive capacity. Large though these numbers look, they are small in relation to the needs of a large country like China. In the 1980s the number of graduates equalled in number to those graduating in the previous three decades. Even so, there is considerable scope for further expansion. At present, tertiary enrolment comes to no more than 2% of the age group cohort.[4]

We can therefore see that even before Deng Xiaoping's reforms got going, China had achieved significant economic progress through Russian assistance in the first decade and by her own efforts thereafter in producing trained manpower. But the economy suffered from the usual weaknesses which all centrally planned systems experienced. Factories were set up by the State and produced goods determined by

---

[4] US National Science Foundation: *Human Resources for Science & Technology: The Asian Region*, 1993, p. 62. By comparison, the figure for India is 5%; Japan, 30%; Singapore, 19%.

the Central Planning Commission. Workers were assigned by the Labour Ministry. They were not free to choose occupations and once assigned to the employing unit, they enjoyed permanent employment. Capital was supplied by state banks according to the central plan. Wages and salaries, prices of goods, interest rates on loans bore no relation to the realities of supply and demand.

The drawbacks of the command economy are known to all of you and I need not elaborate on them. But one element needs to be emphasized. This concerns the ideology that dominated thinking on. important policy issues. To name some items in the ideological menu — the working class (or proletariat) forms the most advanced section of society; a socialist society is superior to a capitalist state; the means of production must be owned by the State. A socialist society is run on a political system embodying what is termed "democratic centralism". This means that the Communist Party holds supreme power and within the Party, authority is vested in the Party's Politburo, a handful of leaders. That was the way the revolution was won and that was the way China was governed between 1949 and 1979. Even today, one can say that the political system remains essentially the same even though there have been no less than four revisions of the Constitution.

The Third Plenary Session of the Eleventh Central Committee held in December 1978, was a landmark event. Under Deng Xiaoping's leadership, China took the first steps towards loosening rigid central controls over production. The first efforts were directed at agricultural production and peasant families were allowed some choice of what to produce once their quota obligations were met. The system, called "contract responsibility system", was later extended to state industrial enterprises.

At the same time, provincial governments were given more authority and this delegation down to the lowest tier of government — the township government — had the intended effect in promoting local initiative. At the same time, central planning controls over allocation of supplies were gradually relaxed. Output above the limit set in state plans could be sold at higher prices. Thus a two-tier price system emerged. The relaxation of controls over prices and production occurred gradually and not in the so-called "Big Bang" fashion adopted in Russia after the break-up of the Soviet Union. Even as late as 1992, 30% of consumer goods (in terms of value of sales) and 42% of industrial raw materials remained under state control, that is, some government official decided who could obtain supplies at planned prices.[5] The level beyond which enterprises could sell at higher market prices became a matter of bargaining between the enterprise managements and the agency supervising them.

Despite these complications, the result of Deng's economic reforms has been a growth of the economy in the last 15 years that must be considered spectacular by any standard. Whereas her former mentor, the Soviet Union, has broken down in an unexpected and dramatic way, China continues to register success after success. But it would be unwise to project the future as a continuation of the past because some deep-seated troubles continue to beset the economy.

These troubles have their origins in the attempts to graft a market economy into a political system that was designed for a different purpose, to manage a command economy. This incompatibility between the requirements of a market economy and the political structure produced set-backs which have yet to be overcome. I briefly mention the more important ones. First is the boom-bust cycle. Marxist dogma asserts that the business cycle is the inherent feature of the capitalist world. But whereas industrial countries have learnt to moderate the business cycle through fiscal and monetary policies, the Chinese have been groping for a solution, so far without much success.

The second problem is even more serious. This concerns the poor performance of most SOEs. Nearly half of them are losing large sums of money. They have to be kept alive by large subsidies from the state budget. Every year Premier Li Peng draws attention to this problem in his address to the National People's Congress. Many kinds of remedies have been tried over the last eight years but to no avail. In a market economy, enterprises which lose money year after year will

---

[5] World Bank, *China: The Achievement and Challenge of Price Reform*, Washington, 1993.

close down. This option is not open to Beijing because this could mean the laying off of some 20 million workers. The leaders believe that the ensuing turmoil will cause an unacceptable level of political instability.

The third of China's unsolved problems could perhaps produce the most dangerous long-term result if it remains unsolved. This is the widespread corruption among those holding positions of authority; given the low salaries which officials get (a product of their ideology), those with authority to grant licences, or supplies at low planned prices, or loans (at negative rates of interest) will need to be saints not to fall to temptation. The redeeming feature is that leaders at the pinnacle of power remain untainted.

The last of the big unsolved problems concerns the progressive weakening of the central government in its dealings with provincial and local governments in industrial, financial and general economic matters. The coastal provinces which have benefited most from the reforms have become increasingly independent of the Centre for funds. In fact, the Centre depends on these provinces to collect revenue on their behalf. Strange though it seems, China practises a kind of tax-farming system used in the later years of the Qing dynasty. One of Vice Premier Zhu Rongji's reforms aims to straighten this matter out by setting up a nation-wide revenue collection system under Beijing's direct control.

Let me discuss this last item — centre-province relationship — at some length as this will give a clear explanation of the consequences of a command-type political system trying to manage a market economy. At first sight, the weakening of the Centre must look an improbable outcome. Supreme power rests with the Party's Central Committee and the Standing Committee of its Politburo exercising this power on its behalf. How could provincial party secretaries and governors disobey the all powerful Politburo? Surely their dismissal would immediately follow. This did happen on many occasions but replacing these office holders seldom solve the problem. Their appointed successors will be exposed to the same pressures to promote the interests of the province, especially to increase its material well-being.

Matters can be complicated when it comes to governing a large country through a system of government which has five layers — centre, provincial, municipal or prefecture, county or township. In all, there are more than 50,000 governments in China. But China's difficulties spring from more than a matter of size. The USA is a large country with the world's largest economy. But the Americans do not experience — trouble in center–local relations. Nor did the former Soviet Union so long as they stuck to the command economy for which their political institutions were designed to manage.

To get to the root of the problem, we must look at China's constitution. The constitution states, "The People's Republic of China is a unitary multinational state built up jointly by the people of all its nationalities." It describes at length the structure of the state, that is, the functions of the People's Congress, the Presidency, the State Council and the Central Military Commission. As regards provincial and local authorities, the constitution states that these are set up directly under the central government. In other words, governments at lower levels may be granted such authority as determined by the Centre. By the same token, authority granted may be withdrawn.

In introducing the market economy in stages, decision-making must also be decentralised in appropriate measure. As economic expansion takes place, conflicts of interest must emerge between the Centre and provinces over a wide range of issues. The sharing of tax revenue is one of the vexatious issues between them. Access to bank loans to build infrastructure turns out to be a zero-sum game played each year by the participants. As the economy grows more complex, both Centre and provinces increasingly engage in off-budget items of revenue and expenditure.

In effect what has happened over the years is that China has effectively become a Federal State as provinces increasingly acquire authority and wealth. As one Chinese scholar observes, post-Mao China has become a Federal State without a Federal Constitution.[6] As a result, both Centre and provinces engage in continuous negotiations

---

[6] Zhao Suisheng, "The Feeble Political Capacity of a Strong One-Party Regime", *Issues and Studies*, Vol. 26, Nos. 1 and 2, January and February 1990.

over issues such as sharing of taxes, control over enterprises sited in provinces, access to bank credit, foreign exchange, imports and exports of goods and a hundred and one items. A Federal Constitution would have defined the limits of authority of provincial governments and unsettled disputes between Centre and provinces could be referred to a Supreme Court. The absence of such a system has given rise to a paradox. Though China has a strong one-party regime, its capacity to formulate and implement economic policy is feeble.

This line of argument shows that much of its current difficulties can be traced to the failure of political reforms to keep pace with economic reforms. This may strike you as a novel and contentious conclusion. But it is not so. As early as 1986, Mr. Deng had been pressing for political reforms, a subject which is seldom discussed today in China.

Let me quote from Mr. Deng's statement made on 3 September 1986: "... our political structure does not meet the needs of economic reform ... Whenever we move one step forward in economic reform we are made keenly aware of the need to change the political structure. If we fail to do that, it will stunt the growth of the productive forces and impede our drive for modernization."[7]

Then, in an independent discovery of Parkinson's law, he said, "At present, leading organs at various levels have so many people on the staff that work has to be found to keep them busy." Mr. Deng had three objectives in mind. The first was to revitalize the Party by enlisting younger, better-educated and more professionally competent cadres. Next, to reduce overstaffing to increase efficiency. Third, to stimulate the initiative at the grass-roots by delegation of authority.[8] Among the shortcomings, he highlighted the need to stop Party cadres from interfering in affairs which lay within the responsibility of the Government. The separation of party and government stood high on his agenda. He also drew attention to the need for a modern legal system, the existing one being flawed especially by failure of enforcement measures.[9]

---

[7] Deng Xiaoping, *Fundamental Issues in Present-day China*, Beijing: Foreign Language Press, 1987, p. 149.
[8] Deng Xiaoping, *op. cit.*, pp. 158–159.
[9] Deng Xiaoping, *op. cit.*, pp. 145–147.

Once the paramount leader had expressed his views in such forthright terms, action soon followed. The Office of Reform of the Political System was set up in September under the direct charge of Prime Minister Zhao Ziyang. In December, seven Special Topic Study Groups were formed, each consisting of between 20 to 30 Party and Government officials as well as scholars drawn from universities and research institutes. The seven topics were:

  (i) Separation of Party and Government.
 (ii) Democracy within the Party.
(iii) Devolution of Authority.
 (iv) Personnel Management.
  (v) Socialist Democracy.
 (vi) Socialist Legal System.
(vii) General Principles of Political Reform.

In June 1987, the seven study groups completed the first drafts of their reports and the following month their proposals were embodied in a document called "General Concept of Political Reform". This document went to the upper reaches of the Party leadership and was eventually adopted by the 13th Party Congress in October 1987.[10]

We need not concern ourselves with the contents of this massive intellectual effort, except to note that it represented a genuine effort by the top leadership to reform the political system. Although in 1988 and 1989 some of the reform measures were initiated, in the end the entire programme was abandoned. What happened was that news of the study groups' deliberations reached staff and students of the universities and provoked much excitement, as to be expected.

Unfortunately, the years 1988/89 witnessed the peak of China's business cycle with its associated high rates of price inflation, exceeding 25% in major cities. University students living on fixed and small stipends were badly affected. Their feelings were

---

[10]Yan Huai, "Zhao Ziyang's Bold Political Reform Attempts at the 13th Party Congress", *IEAPE Background Brief,* July 1994.

aggravated by the sight of people in positions of authority in government and business spending money freely, money which obviously did not come from their meagre salaries. Once discontent became widespread it began to feed on itself. The final result was the Tiananmen tragedy in June 1989.

So far, you may say, this account of major events in post-reform China has been mainly a story of unsolved problems ending in a major political tragedy. How then was the country able to achieve so high a level of economic growth? Why do foreign businessmen get excited? We can say that in the first half of this period, say up to about 1985, the relaxation of controls did produce economic expansion in most sectors of the economy, including state enterprises. These became a burden in the second half of the decade. But something unexpected occurred, unexpected even by Mr. Deng as he admitted, which more than made up for the shortcomings of the state enterprises. This was the extraordinary growth of industry in the countryside.[11]

TVEs are businesses launched mostly by township governments and sometimes by village leaders or even by individual farmers. They are called "rural collective enterprises" to distinguish them from state enterprises and urban collective enterprises. Table 5 shows the enormous expansion of TVEs.

What are the reasons for this unprecedented expansion of a type of enterprise that is unique to China? How could rural folk seize business opportunities on such an extensive scale? How did they get market information and acquire manufacturing know-how? Why did expansion take place in the countryside and not in cities according to the common experience of other countries?[12]

---

[11] Goh Keng Swee, "Growth of Township and Village Enterprises as Result of China's Reforms" (Paper presented for the 1994 *International Herald Tribune/* State Commission for Restructuring Economic System China Summit Meeting); John Wong, "The Quiet Industrial Revolution in the Chinese Countryside: Township and Village Enterprises", *IEAPE Background Brief No. 22*, 3 January 1992.

[12] IEAPE and Beijing University's Sociology Department co-operated in carrying out case studies of 30 TVEs. A book, entitled *Rural Entrepreneurs — Ten Case Studies* written by John Wong, Ma Rong and Tang Mu, was published by Times Academics Press in 1995.

Table 5.   Township and Village Enterprises

	Unit	1978	1984	1992	Increase 1992/1978
Number of TVEs	Million	1.52	6.07	20.92	13.9 times
Workers	Million	28.3	52.1	106.2	3.8 times
Output value	Billion *yuan*	49.5	169.8	17,659.7	35.7 times
Output per worker	*Yuan*	1,752	3,259	16,563	9.5 times

Source: Yearbook of China's TVEs 1993.

There were conditions, some of which existed only in China which explain this phenomenon. One of these was the control over population movement by a nation-wide household registration. The object was to prevent a flood of rural migration to the cities which happened in most Third World countries. Without special permission, people remained where they lived.

The second item was the extensive build-up of production know-how arising from the concentration of studies on engineering and the applied sciences. Most of the engineers worked in cities, mainly in state enterprises. The third arose from the sustained effort in enlarging the scope of the machines-building industries. I have described these in some detail. Even though much of the output did not reach international standards, their prices were low and they could be bought without the use of foreign exchange. Fourth, shortages of goods, especially consumer goods, were a marked feature of the economy and remain so today. This presented a wide choice of products for promoters of TVEs. Finally, surplus labour became a troublesome matter in rural areas. This concentrated the minds of township leaders to find work for them.

When the reforms got going in the early 1980s, the decentralisation policy allowed county and township governments freedom to start enterprises without having to go through a bureaucratic maze to get permits. At first, TVEs concentrated on simple production, such as making building material and simple food processing or providing simple transportation services. After 1984, they entered into more complex production. Here, access to technology and machinery was made possible because these could be obtained from nearby cities. If machinery had to be imported, TVEs could not have got going because of lack of foreign currency. So the enormous effort put into the machine-building industries paid off in a way the planners never expected nor intended. Quite often TVEs engaged city engineers on a part-time basis and when their business prospered, they poached them without hesitation.

In one important respect, the management and operational methods were the opposite of those used in state enterprises. They had to compete to obtain supplies of material inputs as well as in the sale of their outputs. If they lost money they eventually closed down and the workers lost their jobs and went back to the farms. In other words, they operated under a hard budget constraint in a competitive market. By 1992, the output value of TVEs, 1,766 billion yuan, had virtually equalled that of state enterprises, 1,782 billion yuan, and has since surpassed them.

China's rapid economic growth could not have been possible without the great effort made to accumulate knowledge in science and engineering since 1949. When this knowledge was applied in a command economy, the results turned out to be unsatisfactory. Gradual reforms at first produced expansion of output but later brought great strains on the system, because of the rigidities of the political system. The outcome was a number of unsolved problems which I described. These will have to be addressed, perhaps with greater chances of success in the post-Deng era. It was in the rural economy operating outside major political controls that rural enterprises were established under a competitive market environment. These achieved rapid and sustained growth.

Index